APPALACHIAN RURAL HOMELESSNESS:

The Case of Watauga County, North Carolina

NOTE TO THIS EDITION

This edition of this work is the third release, but the first to be made readily available to the public at large. The first release was as a 2008 Thesis for a Masters' program in Appalachian Studies. It sits on assorted academic shelves and was available online for awhile. The second was designed to promote academic studies regarding homelessness throughout Appalachia and was packaged in 2009 as a "Library Edition" including a study by Ian Mance entitled "Homeless in the High Country - A Profile of Homelessness: 1994 -2004." That release made it a bit further afield, being shared with many of those who aided the research and several libraries which seemed to be points where similar research was routinely being started.

Now, as 2015 draws to a close, roughly ten years after the most recent of the activity presented here occurred, I am contemplating performing a follow up study. Much has happened in the realm of homeless service provision, while much has remained the same. Many of the ten year plans to see end homelessness are coming to a close, and many of the central non-local funding entities have tried a variety of ways to encourage strategies that targeted aid to key segments of that population. Indeed, in several instances, the very definitions of homelessness have been changed.

However, a quick round of general searches to find new texts on homelessness in Appalachia and rural areas in general provides no significant change in readily available source material. I am curious to see how all those changes have directed the workflow from region to region, and what has proven successful. I'm also curious to see if my 2009 challenge was met with any increase in locally available research. It may be that a variety of local studies now exist that simple have not made it to a regional review or into the publicly available databases. I realize that not having taken this step sooner greatly limited the availability of my own research, particularly once the website I once maintained was taken down.

I again encourage those positioned to do so to explore conditions, archives, and internal records to make more information available to the student, professional, and lay-person alike about the important street level work that continues on behalf of some of our Nation's most marginalized individuals. My hat is off to all of you who continue to put so much effort into your neighbors and community. Your stories deserve to be told.

There is no significant change in this text from the original version. A variety of formatting effects have been applied to facilitate both publication and readability. Despite all of my previous best efforts new typos and misprints were found and corrected.

Those using portions of this work for educational purposes are welcome to be more relaxed than they would normally be for nonfiction works as they reproduce what they need without additional consent so long as appropriate recognition of source material is maintained, be that myself or those whose efforts I have built upon, and so long as standard lawful practices are still followed for any work that may yield an individual profit.

Thank you to all of the people who care enough to give of their time and resources as they reach out to those in need in compassionate, empathetic, and meaningful ways. I end by reiterating my closing from the 2009 release notes: Thank you for reading; thank you for learning; and most of all, thank you for teaching. It is only in constructive dialogue that we can overcome the ills of society.

Carl Jenkins 12/17/2015

TABLE OF CONTENTS

LIST OF TABLES

LIST OF FIGURES

LIST OF PHOTOGRAPHS

DEDICATION

This work is respectfully dedicated to Reverend James Thompson. His fifteen years as Executive Director of the Hospitality House of Boone are a testament to the need for placing the heart foremost in the provision of care for the victims of homelessness.

COMMON ABBREVIATIONS USED

ADO	Average Daily Occupancy
ARC	Appalachian Regional Commission
BoPC	NC State Board of Public Charities
BoC&PW	NC State Board of Charities and Public Welfare
BoPW	NC State Board of Public Welfare
CAA	Community Action Agency
CCC	Community Cares Clinic
CCC&TI	Caldwell Community College and Technical Institute
	CoalitionHunger Coalition
CoC	Continuum of Care
DSS	Department of Social Services
DV	Domestic Violence
ESG	Emergency Shelter Grant Program
FEMA	Federal Emergency Management Agency
FTE	Full Time Equivalency
GED	General Education Degree
HCUW	High Country United Way
HH	Hospitality House of Boone
HUD	Department of Housing and Urban Development
IRB	Institutional Review Board
IRS	Internal Revenue Service
LW	The Learning Web
MECCA	Methodist, Episcopalian and Catholic Community Action
NCDA	North Carolina Department of Administration
NCSA	North Carolina State Archives
NIMBY	"Not In My Back Yard" attitude
NRBH	New River Behavioral Healthcare
NRHA	Northwestern Regional Housing Authority
OASIS	Acronym used as name; stands for Opposing Abuse with Service Information, and Shelter
OEO	Office of Economic Opportunities
PIT	Point In Time count or survey
REACH	Acronym used as name; stands for Religious Effort to Assist and Care for the Homeless
SA	Salvation Army
TEFAP	The Emergency Food Assistance Program of the USDA
USDA	United States Department of Agriculture
VOC	Volunteer Outreach Center
WAMY	WAMY Community Action; Acronym used in name: WAMY stands for Watauga, Avery, Mitchell and Yancey Counties
WPA	Works Progress Administration
YWCA	Young Women's Christian Association

PREFACE

There are no regional studies of Appalachian homelessness because there are not enough community studies from which to correlate regional trends. This thesis addresses that situation by compiling a history of homeless service provision in Watauga County, North Carolina from archival materials, agency narratives, and community recollections. That community is then compared to other Appalachian examples through site visits, a regional survey, and additional archival materials.

This research discovered that, in the absence of systematic alternatives, local community efforts begun region-wide evolved from grass-roots and faith-based initiatives into federally dependent programs developing along prevailing urban patterns. The majority of successful shelters in Appalachia developed in rural commercial centers already moving towards urban status.

General shelters in the region most often developed during the 1980s in counties with a stable population of around 25,000 or more, offering services to the surrounding counties. Both comprehensive local planning and the necessary population to support a new shelter began to decline after a federally envisioned infrastructure was established and acquisition of fiscal support became more streamlined.

Such shelters remain small in terms of capacity, but have grown large in terms of the scope of needs they address. In addition to shelter and referral services, those needs range from homeless prevention, outreach, and sustenance programs, to follow-up maintenance for former shelter guests. Local shelters have become dependent upon both local networking and federal financing in order to meet the needs of the local homeless and near homeless.

Watauga County maintained its County Home longer than many of its North Carolina neighbors. It was also one of the earliest Appalachian counties in the state to pursue the creation of both a general shelter and a domestic violence shelter. Throughout the county's history, those who have promoted and maintained sheltered care have sought to do so with pride and compassion. At the same time, they have provided a clear example of how local communities have combined with early state and later federal oversight to provide care to the homeless throughout Appalachia. Local shelters, struggling to keep abreast of the needs of a growing population, and while trying to satisfy distant overseers, continue to provide an inadequate response to the needs of Appalachian homeless with no opportunity to explore systemic alternatives.

CHAPTER I

INTRODUCTION

Despite long-standing perceptions of Appalachia as an impoverished region, there has been no study published of homelessness within the region. This is partly because Appalachia has largely been viewed as a rural area, while homelessness has been treated as an urban issue for centuries (Foucault, 1965; Hopper, 1988; Levine, 1981). There is also a tendency to conceptualize both Appalachia and homelessness as homogenous in construct. Where the idea of homelessness has emerged within the region, it has been secondary to significant events involving unforeseen displacements of large numbers of unprepared individuals. No overall study can emerge until studies of day-to-day homelessness in a variety of Appalachian communities become available. This research will begin that process by focusing on the development of homeless service provision in one of those communities and comparing it to data regarding selected programs region-wide, both past and present.

The study of homelessness in primarily rural areas, such as most of Appalachia, has been overlooked and undifferentiated from the expectation of culturally occurring impoverishment. Appalachian social history is full of examples of extreme conditions and events. Several of these have produced large numbers of displaced persons who may or may not thereafter have been recognized as part of the homeless population. Yet, the inability to maintain a home exists as a problem for many individuals within the region even without such events. It is towards those individuals that routine services need to be targeted appropriately.

Watauga County provides an example of Appalachia's struggle to assist such day-to-day homelessness. Such an example is important for communities to be able to draw upon in their efforts to understand and address homelessness. This thesis is a response to the fact that few such examples are publicly available. As a professional service provider in a college town, I have aided countless students conducting a variety of seemingly redundant research projects. However, that research was never made available for furthering similar research, leaving the students unknowingly to retrace each other's footsteps. I hope that future researchers will begin to take the time to make parallel findings from their communities more readily available, and thereby help allow area specific programming to become more efficiently developed and implemented.

It is clear from the research done during this project that the homeless services offered throughout Appalachia develop primarily in areas that are on an urban track or that have already become large cities. Even though most of those services may have been started by groups of citizens concerned with the well being of the less fortunate within their own communities, it is clear that local homeless demographics are moving towards trends evident in larger cities outside the Appalachian region. The original social concerns become complicit in national trends as external oversight introduces factors not yet encountered in smaller communities.

In almost every local situation I have investigated, community concern opened the door for services to be developed and offered. With rare exception, governmental assistance and guidance have been sought and accepted after initial action plans were in place. As each community grows, dependence evolves to rely increasingly upon examples provided by larger and more remote think tanks. The fact remains that programs developed outside the community seldom address locale-specific needs efficiently.

Church coalitions, dedicated individuals, and community forums, often including involvement from various academic faculties, formed the foundation for many of the agencies I visited in Appalachian North Carolina, Maryland, and New York, as well as many of those who responded to a region-wide survey sent to shelter providers in Appalachian counties from Georgia, North Carolina, Ohio, Tennessee, and West Virginia. The primary service providers for the homeless and at risk populations currently operating in Watauga County all have similar beginnings. Such agencies evolved through community concerns, interests, and actions, but succeeded partly due to fiscal aid and professional standards available from less connected governmental organizations.

Currently, community action agencies (CAAs), housing authorities administering Department of Housing and Urban Development (HUD) programs, the American Red Cross, Departments of Social Services (DSS), some unit of behavioral health coordination, and a variety of faith-based groups appear region-wide to be the most consistently available avenues of support for those in need. Together they offer a framework within which other agencies grow and develop as needs arise. In some areas, they more readily shoulder the responsibility for meeting emerging needs than in others. In almost all areas, their presence in early discussions will often render the identification of gaps in services a much more efficient process. If there is a local university or a strong local school district involved, various departments within them often prove helpful at various stages. None of these agencies should be expected to espouse an holistic view on their own. In fact, large agencies either need to be locally active or locally benign. To put it bluntly, if such large agencies do not bear direct responsibility for providing services, they can only be effective as advisors, not as leaders. They do not share appropriate levels of direction and purpose to be thrust into such a role. Each community will have different groups who are capable of taking on such responsibility.

Where facilities for homeless individuals are concerned, there has always been external accountability as to what and how services are offered in Watauga County. The "county home model" of sheltered indigent care – long promoted by federal and state governments (Chancellor, 1901; Yates, 1901) – was adopted locally in the late nineteenth century, once local demand became great enough to warrant general sheltered support (See Appendix A.) The Board of Volunteers most often filed reports upon request,[1] and facility upgrades were made when it was observed as necessary by the County Commission. When an increase in specialized state institutional services required relocation of "inmates," they were dutifully remanded for specialized care. In addition, when the New Deal era programs of the early-1930s effectively eliminated the requirement of the county almshouse in favor of a regional shelter system, Watauga County allowed its own County Home to dwindle and close (Watauga County, 1960).

Although this thesis explores homeless service provision in Appalachia, the region never was as isolated nor as homogenous as common stereotype once claimed. Even once sufficient numbers of community homeless studies are available, it will be difficult to identify regional trends. Some of the policies and practices that have emerged have been directly or indirectly attributable to a variety of external activities. As the primary locus of research is Watauga County, North Carolina, I have not tried to uncover how every state overlapping Appalachia has contributed to the treatment of the homeless. The following sections introduce how various regions have overlapped in the development of homeless service provision.

National Context

At the root of homeless service provision in the United States is a collection of practices focused on addressing a variety of marginal populations, known as the Poor Laws, which began evolving in Europe

---

[1] See the glossary for definitions of terms that may be unclear in this text.

from the sixteenth through the eighteenth centuries. A wealth of information exists on how those laws evolved throughout America's early history. The crux of the system is that local communities were responsible for taking care of anyone not able to care for themselves or to be cared for by their families. Early American cities either depended upon charitable organizations to provide such care, or developed their own almshouses and asylums for the purpose. As the nation coalesced, the county emerged as the primary unit of residency with the responsibility for providing such care as proved necessary, usually through either general fund assistance, known as "outdoor relief," or placement of inmates in the care of county homes. A partial summary of poor law evolution is included in Appendix A.

Additionally, it is well recognized that urban and rural areas do not integrate equally into the economic structure that has precipitated federal homeless policy. It has not been well accepted, even if it is understood, that urban and rural differences require different approaches when it comes to managing homelessness. Although communities usually develop services in response to local need, they are then encouraged to move progressively towards upholding governmentally envisioned standards as a means to retain funding. Those standards pre-suppose a commonality among all program beneficiaries with clearly recognizable variations.

The "county home model" was adopted in the New England states, where much of the un-intentional experimentation of methods was undertaken well before most Southern states determined need for a response. New York State was tracking demographics in the early nineteenth century almost at the level of individual townships (Yates, 1901). At the same time, Maryland was already promoting specialized state facilities (Chancellor,1901). Although the end of the Civil War prompted action, North Carolina really did not begin active involvement with such facilities until after the turn of the twentieth century (North Carolina State Board of Public Charities (NCSBoPC), 1912).

Throughout the development of indigent care, there was a constant struggle to achieve a balance between individual rights and the responsibility of communities to take care of their citizenry. As individual rights to self-determination gained ground, the sense of community duty deteriorated, especially in the areas of greatest population, where economic standing had surpassed subsistence skills as a measure of an individual's community worth (Levine, 1981). Ultimately, the federal government would step in to attempt to regain balance by promoting access to both self-sufficiency and economic opportunities, while largely eliminating social responsibilities based on legal residency. Large cities emerged as centers of economic opportunity along with federally promoted transient shelters.

Today, many agencies have demonstrated that participation with governmental guidance is acceptable by receiving federal funds in exchange for adopting standardized practices and policies of detailed demographic documentation. To be sure, regular refinements and fiscal reevaluations of the grants have offered enough periodic stress to make agency directors question that decision regularly, but location in supportive if not affluent communities combines with generally appreciative clients to offer encouragement for many Appalachian service providers to keep up the work, and the subservience.

Even before the formation of the Appalachian Regional Commission (ARC) in the mid-1960s, and continuing on through the development of programs under HUD and the Office of Economic Opportunities (OEO), the federal government strove to include community specific needs in assistance programs by asking communities to identify local projects that needed funding within broad parameters. Over time, most of those broad parameters where homelessness is concerned have constricted to the level of choosing from a short list of options, despite the creation of local Continuums of Care (CoC) to facilitate progress.

Such CoCs distribute available funds and coordinate, with varying levels of efficiency, the regional creation of programs that target specific classes within the homeless population of their districts. Ideally, a CoC board is comprised of individuals from various segments of the local community including governments, involved faith-based groups, potential donors, and potential organizational recipients of the funds. Input from past or potential individual beneficiaries is desirable. In practice, those active at the meetings for most CoCs only represent those who are actively receiving HUD and OEO grants. Far too much staff activity is spent every year on several levels justifying the need for continued funding for the process to be efficient. Most CoCs are robbed of time and energy needed to expand their spheres of influence into addressing the underlying causes of homelessness addressed by their constituent agencies, and thereby in reversing the process.

Throughout much of American history, it has been very common public sentiment to blame the victim for one's own homelessness if a simpler more definite cause was not readily available –such as a house fire or an abusive partner. By the early and mid-1980s, systematic guidance for homelessness was still primarily sought federally – a legacy of the days of the Great Depression and the War on Poverty. Because New Deal era programs initially designed to be temporary became permanent, federal policy was concurrently an active part of the problem, and just beginning to think constructively again about what could be done – largely from a mental health perspective, in the aftermath of Deinstitutionalization.

Such federal ambiguity helped to trigger the upsurge of shelter development partially through its promotion of economically focused policies that widened the socio-economic gap, allowing an increase among those unable to sustain a livelihood. Compounding the situation was the subsequent recognition that there existed sub-populations among the homeless not adequately served by non-profit and big-city shelters. Although it was commonly recognized by the public that Deinstitutionalization had not progressed as planned, the ramifications were not universally interpreted or accepted, leaving cities, towns, and counties to posit their own unguided, or even misguided, solutions, while trying to satisfy federal practices.

In the early 1990s, the federal government was ready to start offering grants and guidance to compliant shelters. Policy and programming began to develop more consistently and quickly, based largely on what grantors requested and were willing to finance. As community and local government funds were limited, the easiest way to develop a budget was to qualify for as much outside aid as possible. For good and bad, federal aid and other high-justification funding remains the primary means of increasing the budget today. The irony is that where individuals once asked their local governments for aid, local governmental units now ask the federal government for aid with far greater expectations for fiscal justification. Homeless service provision in Appalachia has become a matter of taking available money to offer services rather than seeking ways to provide what is locally in demand.

Ian Mance (2005), a former shelter office manager and Appalachian State University political science masters graduate, found nationally that receiving entitlement benefits frequently does not help recipients rise above the poverty line. He also found nationally, that the largest group of homeless comprised single women, including those with dependent children. Research discussed later will show that this trend is not directly supported by the Appalachian example.

The U.S. House of Representatives documents a 41% increase in the number of impoverished between 1979 and 1990 (Mance, 2005), the same period that gave us Ronald Reagan, no pre-conceived alternatives in the wake of deinstitutionalized mental healthcare, and the emergence of shelter services in almost every surveyed community now offering such services. Such a rapid increase in shelter services demonstrates that many included in that 41% rise in poor became homeless.

Mance (2005) cites studies by Vissing and the National Coalition of Homelessness (NCH) stating that poverty rates are worse in rural areas, where the homeless also tend to be a higher percentage White racially and often first time homeless victims. The U.S. Bureau of the Census, cites Mance, provided statistics giving a non-metro poverty rate in 1998 of 15.9% compared to a rate of 12.6% for urban areas and a 13.3% for the nation. There exists the potential for the rural rate to be even higher due to the reduced attention paid to abandoned structures in those areas, which allows a population of hidden rural homeless. The notion is supported by the personal knowledge of Appalachian service providers working with individuals who lived in old barns and similar structures and only occasionally came by the shelter for meals, showers, and sometimes mail (Mance, 2005).

Furthermore, many of the homeless in cities are there because there were no adequate options for assistance available in their own, more rural, communities (Grand, 2001; Hopper, 2003). Many suffering in rural areas are overlooked because outreach is harder to implement in areas where avoiding public scrutiny is easier to achieve. Vissing (1996) also found that, although overall per capita welfare spending was also roughly equivalent in areas where services were available, rural areas saw a significant portion of that funding spent on agriculturally based programs that facilitated economic progress rather than local welfare.

The former county home model of service provision was not without its share of inefficiencies and inconsistencies, but it initially recognized that it was better to first seek provision for the homeless in the same localities as their support networks. This is still true today, especially in rural areas where the majority of the victims of homelessness have not yet been caught up in the cycle of system failure and inadequate response to need.[2] It was not until states began to enforce their claims of oversight responsibility that the focus shifted towards economic responsibilities.

Although this thesis will not completely address the issue of such displaced care, the case of Watauga County can demonstrate several positives and negatives of system response that have emerged during the County's history and urbanization. To be clear, this thesis also does not support the idea that victims of homelessness should only seek opportunities in home communities as once was required by the

---

[2] That cycle is often called 'a revolving door' as clients graduate from a shelter only to find that they really were not yet stable enough to make it on their own. As people become comfortable with a lower quality of life, they stop putting effort into succeeding and start going through the motions that they have found keep them in good standing with agencies assisting them.

outmoded poor laws (Bureau of the Census & Labor, 1906). Opportunities exist not only in one's home communities, but also in communities that are familiar or even completely new to the individual, but mesh with one's skills and other needs. At the same time, the assumption should not be made that relocation would be best for a homeless individual based on apparent health or behavior patterns alone, and definitely not solely because it is not easy to bring services to those who need them.

North Carolina

To properly understand Watauga County's position, it is necessary to understand how the state managed legislation and programming prior to the current level of services. From the latter half of the eighteenth century through the mid nineteenth century, the state of North Carolina sporadically adopted statewide laws that did little more than make official various aspects of old poor laws (Brown, 1928; Bureau of the Census & Labor, 1906).

Following the Civil War, when the United States solidified as a single nation, North Carolina, as a former Confederate state, was required to submit an updated constitution that was satisfactory to the Union. The new 1868 State Constitution outlined a public responsibility to help those poor who could not help themselves, and mandated that a board be set up with the responsibility of overseeing the implementation of such responsibility. Article 11, Section 7 of the State Constitution stated:

> Beneficent provision for the poor, the unfortunate and orphan, being one of the first duties of a civilized and Christian State, the General Assembly shall, at its first session, appoint and define the duties of a Board of Public Charities, to whom it shall be entrusted the supervision of all charitable and penal State institutions, and who shall annually report to the Governor upon their condition, with suggestions for their improvement. (NCSBoPC, 1870)

That same Constitution would firm up the remainder of the basic poor laws as they would remain little changed until the Great Depression and the subsequent New Deal programs. The constitutional quote would appear in every volume of the Board of Public Charities and its successor Boards' reports.

The Board of Public Charities was thus formed and provided its first official report in 1870. Since the Board was not allotted funds with which to perform its work, there was not another report printed until

1889. Thereafter, despite regular observations of inadequate funds, the Board printed a report through 1916, when a recommendation to increase its authority led to a change in name and functional focus (NCSBoPC, 1917; North Carolina State Board of Charities and Public Welfare (NCSBoC&PW), 1918).

The 1876 halt to the legal practice of "letting" paupers (Brown, 1928) also indirectly lets us know that some factions of state leadership were already beginning to recognize the right to self-determination that later played a major part in the Deinstitutionalization process of the mid-twentieth century. Prior to that legislation, caregivers could "let," or rent out the labor of, a pauper in their care to someone else without wage compensation (Brown, 1928), much as slave owners a generation before were wont to do with their own wards (Dunaway, 2003). The justification was that the pauper was thereby contributing to his or her own upkeep, just as workhouses justified their own forced labor.

The process of individualizing emancipation continued when in "1891 an attempt had been made to remove the stigma implied in the name by enacting that the county institution for the care of the poor no longer should be known as the "poorhouse," but should be designated and provided for as 'the home for the aged and infirm'" (Brown, 1928, p. 70). Despite adopting the name, it would not be until the 1940s that remaining County Homes would adopt the elderly as their primary focus, and by then they were little more than outdated facilities and ill-kept nursing homes.

Although it was clear during this research that State Board members in North Carolina were often ignorant of and/or unresponsive to the variety of communities encompassed within their oversight, the social realities of the home county of each was not explored by this study. Most of their homes were outside Appalachia's borders. It is apparent that social realities of those counties containing a variety of state institutions suggested to resident State Board members that the elderly constituted all that still needed the care of the old Homes.

The reports of the North Carolina State Board of Public Charities demonstrated that County Homes generally only reported if inmates were "able" or "not able." A cursory review of the reports to the Board collected in any year indicates that some responders presumed such ability referred to the ability to help the Keeper's family around the farm, and that some presumed that the designation referred to the inmates' potential to leverage their own skills towards eventual discharge.

As the original Board evolved, the reports themselves become clearly biased towards the professional experiences of each successive State Board's members, who were frequently drawn from the staffs of state-run facilities. Such facilities specialized in single marginalizing factors such as blindness, mental illness, or veteran status, among others, and sought to gather all such individuals from within a broad region together for focused treatment. In addition to providing the services they deemed valuable, such board members clearly wanted to increase funding available to their employers by increasing observable demand, reducing per capita costs to those institutions and to the county, and thereby demonstrate the fiscal value of state institutions over county level ones. That the overall per capita cost of the new, largely administrative, state-based system spanning local, state, and federal levels was vastly higher than the county-based system being outmoded was overlooked completely in reports as presented to the General Assembly.

Reports to the Board of Public Charities on the various County Homes were usually provided to the County Commission by a local representative or by a volunteer system of county visitors. In and around Watauga County, the Superintendant of Health tended to lead the volunteers on visits for the purpose of reports to both the State Board and the County Commissioners. The Superintendant frequently acted as well as the default physician for both the jail and Home. Prior to the system of county visitors, the reality of routine state inspections was greatly diminished roughly in relation to each county facility's proximity to a state institution or an inspector's home. Although state representatives did not become available more often, the routine established through county visitors' reports promoted more official local standards. It also facilitated biased state comparisons.

Despite obvious attempts, county report numbers did not always add up as published in the Board reports. Some of the apparent reasons were a misunderstanding of the time frames to be reported upon, a local desire to get the forms done, the seasonal fluctuations of guests staying part of the year at state institutions,[3] or bias to the partially understood and divergent desires of the various members of the Board.

The transfiguration of the Board of Public Charities into the Board of Charities and Public Welfare followed closely in the wake of a 1915 U. S. Supreme Court ruling that essentially expanded upon and made nationally universal the idea long espoused by several states that County Homes were a necessary expense that did not require a vote of the people to be determined locally necessary. This allowed bonds to be

---

[3] One Watauga County report catalogued in the state record declares that the occupancy of the home was "Thirteen, and during the summer months fourteen, when a blind girl returns from the state school" (NCSBoPC, 1910, p. 91).

issued as necessary by County Commissions for the construction of said facilities. North Carolina had already adopted a similar stance in 1785 (Brown, 1928).

Beginning in 1917 (NCSBoC&PW, 1918), the newly restyled North Carolina State Board of Charities and Public Welfare focused most of its attention on state institutions and related program statistics, generally relegating County Homes to a couple of pages of statewide summary and pessimistic highlights of negative stories in support of the broader platforms being lobbied any given year. For example, the 1922 report promoted the stance that caring for the feeble minded in the unspecialized local shelters only allowed them to breed more feeble minded, thus more state institutions were needed (NCSBoC&PW, 1922).

Giving more space than ever before or after in North Carolina to the analysis of County Homes, the 1922 report identified several instances of multiple generations in a family classed as feeble minded. Playing to the racial fears of the time, the report sought out examples whereby offspring were of mixed racial origin, along with those who resulted from interactions of County Home inmates with those of prison work camps. The report is full of contemporary photos of individuals who fit the stereotypes of familial inbreeding, racial inter-breeding, and mental retardation.

The collective Board of Charities and Public Welfare reports also demonstrated a preferred focus on families and children and the increased specialization and centralization of facilities. They argued that such facilities, although initially expensive to create, would save money in the long run as counties could spend less each year making payments to new facilities that did not require as much physical upkeep and by making multi-county agreements to house the small remainder – those ineligible for specialized centralization – in a shared facility. This would allow outdated facilities to be closed, sold, and returned to the county tax rolls (NCSBoC&PW, 1924).

In so doing, the state made clear its stance that regional urban centers were the way of the future, with little regard for the value of the families and extended social networks left behind by those in need. The various counties, however, did not buy into the multi-county concept until state institutions reduced the number of locally sheltered inmates to levels that made the Homes seem unnecessary, or at least unprofitable and un-sustainable for prospective Keepers seeking a livelihood. County Commissions were also often faced with badgering from the State Board to renovate those Homes to either meet the standards of examples found in more affluent parts of the state, or close them down.

Along with the restructuring of the Board of Public Charities was the creation of the County Superintendent of Public Welfare, a post frequently added to the job description of the pre-existing Superintendent of Education (Brown, 1928). Administratively, this was a move that made certain that state supervision was almost purely a desk job. Much as absentee ownership has done nationally, this only served to desensitize those making decisions to the variety of communities served, and encouraged them to derive their impetus from examples observed in larger urban settings where their offices were generally located. North Carolina was rushing to emulate other states (Noll, 1995) already backing away from locally operated facilities after post-Civil War national concerns were abated and new conflicts were capturing public attention.

Legislation in 1923 introduced the Mothers' Aid program to benefit indigent mothers with young children. The program partially addressed the perceived need for increased oversight of outdoor relief practices in many locales (Brown, 1928). It also began in earnest the process of differentiating various types of non-institutionally-based welfare. Such differentiation relegated poorhouse statistics to decreasing priority for reporting purposes, making homeless population numbers increasingly hard to find. Mothers' Aid effectively marked the beginning of an increased public awareness of prevention as a response to homelessness, which reduced the trend of social disenfranchisement as a requirement of receiving aid. The poor could now be helped while they were still participating in the community.

Analyzing the New Deal era programs applied in North Carolina, Annie O'Berry states that "Prior to 1932, relief of destitution was a minor phase of governmental activity in North Carolina. Each County provided, through public funds, for its own indigents – mostly the aged and infirm – by outside poor relief, or in County Homes" (O'Berry, 1936, p. 22). It is notable that administrative situations did not really improve after the 1936 publication of O'Berry's findings. She does go on, in the same paragraph (p. 22), to state, "In general, needy and unfortunate persons were aided through churches, private organizations, and charitable agencies – from funds contributed by individuals." North Carolina clearly deemed the welfare of its individual citizens to be the responsibility of the private sector.

Although O'Berry's study is a wonderfully detailed and thorough review of a rather complex set of programs, the crux is that North Carolina dutifully provided the requisite oversight personnel for New Deal programs and relatively efficiently administered the funds made available by the federal government between 1932 and 1935 in accordance to its rapidly changing stipulations. It did all this while diligently pursuing all opportunities to avoid providing matching state funds and ultimately came through without spending a penny from its own coffers on emergency relief. The state applied such thrift where it could to minimize what turned out to be a top-heavy administrative component, and diligently pursued molding the available federal programs to North Carolina's variations of the nation's woes (O'Berry, 1936). Compassion was thus never backed by state budget.

Governor Oliver Max Gardner had created the Governor's Council on Unemployment and Relief in December of 1930. The Council's purpose, until it became obsolete in June of 1932, was to study statewide poverty issues and to create a plan of action. Since a federal plan was implemented in July 1932, before the Council had presented an action plan, it cannot be known what that Council may have led the state to do (O'Berry, 1936).

The various counties were less fortunate than the state in preserving their own funds. Echoing the findings of Mrs. O'Berry, Ellen Winston, as the Commissioner of the North Carolina Board of Public Welfare, would later state:

> Thousands of citizens between 16 and 65 years of age who are unemployable through illness, physical or mental handicap, or lack of any skill are dependent upon inadequate county appropriations for general assistance. There are no State funds to help such people. On all programs of financial assistance North Carolina ranks near the bottom. (North Carolina State Board of Public Welfare (NCSBoPW), 1948a, p. 16)

While stressing a need to promote preventive services and organization of efforts on the community level, Winston went on to say:

> It is believed that the time has come when the State should provide its share of the funds necessary to meet subsistence needs of all persons, regardless of age, who are dependent upon public support. In comparison with the fiscal effort of other States, North Carolina falls far short in State efforts to provide financial assistance to needy citizens. (NCSBoPW, 1948a, p. 17)

In light of Winston's position and her willingness to include such statements in her introduction to the report presented to the North Carolina General Assembly, it was clearly known to legislators of the day that North Carolina had long avoided responsibility for direct response to general homelessness.

Despite a national awakening to homeless groups as subsets of the impoverished during the Depression, differentiation of homeless individuals from other aid recipients in the public record is impossible to research after around 1940. North Carolina simply was not concerned with tracking the numbers of the homeless until the current shelter system began to evolve in the late 1970s in various localities out of nationally unanswered public concerns. Those concerns were generated primarily by two interwoven nationally involved events: mental health Deinstitutionalization and the Vietnam Conflict (Tollett, 1992).

It is well documented that wartime job markets and the draft contributed to the decline in the national levels of visible homeless individuals (Tollett, 1992). Since non-sheltered aid was long tied to the availability of a mailing address (Hopper, 2003), it is quite possible that very little help was given to anyone truly homeless between the closure of County Homes and the opening of regional shelters, except that which was available from county or city coffers, or from charitable organizations like the American Red Cross or the Salvation Army.

Even the North Carolina Fund, launched by Governor Sanford in 1963 to target poverty, saw efforts of its community agencies focused on impoverished homeowners, educational shortfalls, and racial issues. Sanford, despite his position as Governor, had to seek funding for his program from the private sector instead of the State Legislature, receiving the program's initial funding from the Ford Foundation (Cerese & Channing, 2008).

Since programs like Mothers' Aid are inherently preventive in focus, it is possible that homelessness was initially reduced. Fiscally strained family relationships should have been partially ameliorated through what was essentially increased and publicly tailored outdoor aid. Tracking of homelessness, in the absence of state reporting, was relegated to the various localities' whims on public disclosure. No data were uncovered during this research to support or refute an actual decline in homelessness in either North Carolina or Watauga County as a result of those preventive measures. Certainly, by the mid-1970s, the need for a local shelter was at least as great as it had ever been around the turn of the century. Shelters were beginning to open in the more populous rural areas, while other communities were starting the planning process.

For the most part, North Carolina has contented itself to act as a bridge between federal and local programming, attempting to compile demographic data in various fashions with varying success at efficiency since the conclusion of the Civil War. North Carolina's direct contribution to the reduction of homelessness has been greatest for various sub-groups of the high-risk and clearly incidental homelessness sufferers, such as domestic violence (DV) victims, widows of veterans, or foster care programs. The institutions for these services were most often provided at the partial expense of the sufferers' counties of origin.

Mental Illness Among Homeless

Mental illness cannot be neglected when looking at those who have become homeless, especially among those with addictive behaviors. A brief explanation of how mental illness, substance abuse, and homelessness intersect will provide background for exploring the data.

The power allowed various State Board members, both in North Carolina and elsewhere, demonstrates that institutionalization practices comprised social action, and that segregation based on health issues was physical as well as mental in nature. Although feeble mindedness was afforded a high degree of stigma, it was long deemed a factor of either overall physical constitution or education, if not both. Mental health did not truly become a separate social concern until after World War I efforts advanced understanding of a variety of mental afflictions through the evaluation of officers and veterans (Levine, 1981).

The aftermath of Deinstitutionalization made it clear that, at least socially, those who were less mentally or emotionally capable were to be lumped together with those who were enfeebled through trauma as a marginal segment of society. Since mental ailments cannot be quantified by the layman in the way that physical ailments, such as a missing leg, can be, the emergence of professionals qualified to evaluate such issues precipitated the emergence of perceived responsibility to address all such individuals accordingly.

As a complicating factor among the homeless, mental illness has been observed as a problem for many years (Hopper, 1988; Snow, Baker, & Martin, 1986; Talley & Coleman, 1992; Wright, 1988). In my professional observation, there are two reasons today for its prevalence: (1) the legacy of Deinstitutionalization, and (2) the desire to quickly affix blame to the victim.

There is no doubt that there are many individuals who are mentally ill. There is also no doubt that a variety of situations that can arise in life render many of those individuals more susceptible to falling into homelessness. Where once they were locked away in institutions and not allowed the opportunity to do what they could for themselves, now they are effectively locked out and have to potentially over-reach themselves in order to develop or exploit alternative opportunities to have accomplished that which they cannot do for themselves.

The cultural tendency of making individuals responsible for all of the problems that come their way has made it easy for those finding themselves in any critical situation, including homelessness, to be diagnosed as mentally ill (Hopper, 1988). While an inability to cope once made it easy to justify locking an individual away, those now providing services recognize that they are working with a variety of conflicting life choices and situations. They still prefer that those accessing their services act rationally in order to make the process more efficient. Although most of us have learned a level of bottling things inside that allows us to provide a level of courtesy in our everyday dealings, finding oneself homeless is not an everyday situation for the majority of its victims; it is an emergency for most people, and rational behavior is hard to maintain during irrational events. This is especially true when an individual barely yet able to grasp what has just happened is confronted with someone expecting him (or her) to parse his life and current experiences along with his needs in accord with a list of preconceived questions and answers of which the individual is unaware.

Emergency management tells us to expect those experiencing an emergency to behave irrationally (Landesman, 2001). Yet, service providers often require those reacting irrationally to becoming homeless to access behavioral health services based on their temporary reactions, rather than their normal actions. Mental health services then evaluate presented behaviors and thoughts to determine the status of one's normal mental health. Such evaluation frequently includes exploration of indicators for mental health disorders early on as there may only be one meeting available for needs assessment.

Mental health professionals strive to include situation in their evaluation, but, when the situation does not quickly go away, or the individual cannot be distracted from that situation, identifying the normal state becomes difficult. Thus, a person can effectively become mentally ill only because they are homeless. If behaviors or drugs are prescribed, or otherwise taken, to counter the diagnosis, an alternate balance is introduced to the situation, which leaves the homeless victim with yet another new theme to focus on in order to regain a life of stability. Discontinuing or interrupting that treatment can further disrupt the balance as the body and mind try to reassert natural perspective.

Substance abuse can be similarly viewed. I found in my time working with the homeless that alcohol abuse was split fairly evenly between those who were homeless because they were alcoholics, and those who were using alcohol as a coping mechanism, either to becoming homeless, or to other underlying issues that ultimately led to both homelessness and alcoholism. In the case of the first group, when addicts were able to set aside alcohol long enough to experience a level of success, they usually backslid. They usually believed themselves to be among the coping only set, or at least wanted everyone, including themselves, to so believe.

Although lapses of reason may have gone along with initial tastes of renewed success among the copers, the dependence on alcohol usually disappeared as continued small successes renewed their self-esteem and they redeveloped faith in themselves. Alcohol may have continued to be used as a stress reliever, but not to the detriment of livelihood and no more than many successful members of society. Sometimes, the opportunity to quit alcohol altogether is seized; at other times, the need to set usage aside for the sake of others sharing an institutional setting is hard to understand. The casual drunk simply does not understand the addiction of the true alcoholic.

Although I saw countless successes among the copers, true addicts rarely succeeded among the general homeless. Indeed, even local substance abuse treatment facilities like Serenity Farms and Hebron Colony both struggled with high rates of failure, especially among those that did not maintain a continued network of recovery support after graduating the programs. Virtually all hard drug users and most of those abusing prescription drugs were truly addicted.

The only success story among homeless alcoholics that sticks in my mind is of one individual I worked with off and on for several years. He claimed to have been through alcohol detoxification centers over forty times as well as several recovery programs before a non-personal emergency in his family finally caused him to rethink his priorities. The last time I saw him he had been sober for over three years, primarily by placing the needs of family above his own.

Although recognizing substance abuse patterns and mental or physical health issues can provide useful information in helping clients overcome homelessness, the labels that go along with such patterns are often ways through which people are made to feel marginalized by their communities. This is especially true if they are trying to work within a program that is poorly able to help with their key issues. One key to success in overcoming most obstacles is to feel connected and supported. Substance abuse programs such as Alcoholics Anonymous, and halfway houses such as Watauga County's Serenity Farms and Hebron Colony, as well as many other programs focused on a variety of marginalizing issues, are valuable not only to recovering from an addiction, but also in regaining and retaining stability when returning to the community through connection with a supportive and understanding social network.

The current shelters in Watauga County's history have always kept abreast of what programs exist locally at any given time in order to make sure that their clients were able to address as many of their obstacles to housing stability as possible. Both Hospitality House and OASIS have routinely provided or facilitated an assortment of support groups, skills groups, and even at times groups based on recreational activities, allowing residents and other clientele to briefly set aside problems and just enjoy activities such as gardening, writing, foreign language, or sewing.

Agencies Explored

A variety of agencies and organizations have been researched during this project. Although many others are throughout the following chapters, I will introduce some of the primary ones before moving on to the chapter describing the various methods employed in my research.

The oldest facilities that I have examined closely are former County Homes. These shelters provided a loosely defined program to an even more loosely defined clientele. In general, those that sought or were remanded to such assistance were either infirm according to contemporary ideology, or were without remaining family or friends to help care for them, be they elderly, orphaned, widowed, ill, or otherwise incapable of self-sufficiency. Usually, those who were able either followed their own plan towards a return to self-sufficiency, or helped the Keeper of the County Home on the farm or around the house. I have studied the Watauga County Home most closely, but have given more than casual attention to several others, including one in Tompkins County, New York, and to those elsewhere in Appalachian North Carolina.

Hospitality House of the Boone Area, Inc. in Watauga County provides services to all homeless or at-risk individuals through a soup kitchen and several levels of shelter programming. The Hunger and Health Coalition in Watauga County, provides services through a food pantry, a variety of prescription and screening programs, and winter assistance, including firewood and holiday programming. OASIS, Inc. – which stands for Opposing Abuse through Services, Information, and Shelter – also located in Watauga County, offers a full spectrum of domestic violence and sexual abuse services, including shelter. The Watauga Crisis Assistance Network (WeCAN) offers finance-based crisis assistance and homelessness prevention services to Watauga County residents. These agencies and their programs are discussed in detail in the chapter focused on Watauga County.

In addition to the programs in Watauga County, visits to two other Appalachian Counties allowed for more in-depth evaluation of regional programs. The REACH program in Hagersville, Maryland is a cold-weather shelter that offers year round assistance to those out on the streets, including laundry, showers, light meals, and guidance. It is the only one of several shelters in the city that does not enforce a required period of residency to qualify for sheltered services. The only shelter in Tompkins County, New York, is also one of only a handful of emergency shelters operated by the American Red Cross nationwide. It is also quite integrated with an extensive pantry system and works closely with a homeless outreach program operated by Learning Web. Learning Web provides a variety of services for teens and younger adults. These communities are described in more detail in the chapter on Appalachia.

All of these agencies work closely with various other programs in their areas targeting homeless prevention through job training, crisis assistance, behavioral health programs, medical and nutrition assistance, and housing assistance. None of them would be effective without the networking afforded by these agencies or a variety of volunteers coming from either local universities or faith groups. The Salvation Army also currently has a varying degree of presence in all three communities studied.

The first step in community response to everyday homelessness should be to look at one's own community. Since there remains very little publicly available documentation of such community response, except in larger cities, the bulk of this thesis will address that issue in Watauga County, North Carolina. Parallels and comparisons are drawn from other Appalachian community responses when feasible.

CHAPTER II

METHODS OF RESEARCH

The two objectives of this research were first to compile a chronology of the evolution of homeless service provision in Watauga County, North Carolina, and then to juxtapose the resultant example to others within the Appalachian experience in order to allow a study of regional homelessness to begin to emerge. This chapter will describe how I have carried out the research.

In order to develop a chronology of the provision of services to the homeless of Watauga County, North Carolina, it has been necessary to combine several methods of research. Those methods include interviews with past and current members of the community, the internal records of some of the current agencies, local newspapers, and the archival record generated by county and state agencies. Over a decade of personal experience with the homeless, primarily as a service provider, also adds perspective to my findings.

Watauga County is viewed in the Appalachian regional perspective through comparison of those same resources from outside the county, additional site visits, and a mailed survey of regional organizations offering shelter. I have adopted the boundaries of Appalachia as currently defined by the Appalachian Regional Commission (ARC).

ARC was formed by the Conference of Governors in 1965 as part of the War on Poverty in order to address high levels of poverty in an area seen as culturally distinctive, primarily through economic development. Today, Appalachia is comprised of 410 counties in 13 states running southwest from southern New York to northern Mississippi. The region of Appalachia is named after the primary mountain range it overlays. It includes parts of New York, Pennsylvania, Ohio, Maryland, Virginia, Kentucky, North Carolina, Tennessee, South Carolina, Georgia, Alabama, Mississippi, and all of West Virginia.

As discussed in the introduction, the idea of Appalachia has emerged as the embodiment of rural America, while treatment of homelessness has emerged within an urban response towards various marginalized populations. Since this thesis focuses on homeless service provision in an Appalachian community, the research requires some juxtaposition of urban and rural values.

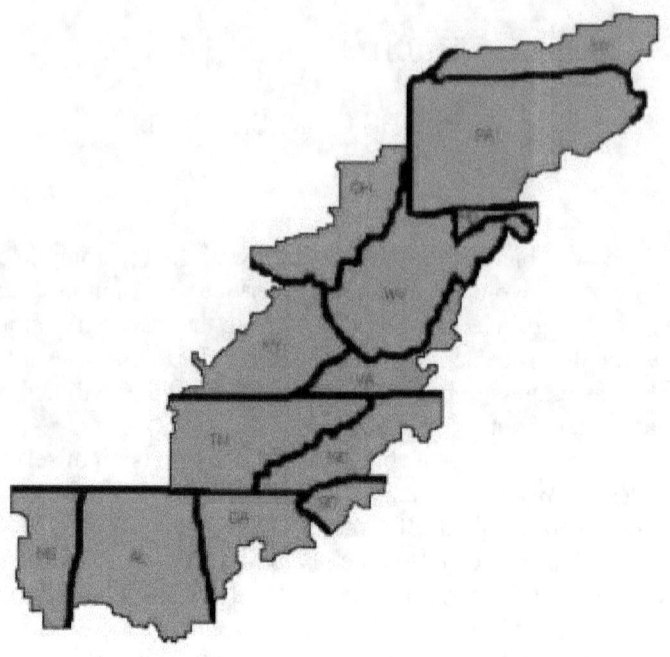

Figure 1: *Map of Appalachia.*

For the purposes of this research, I have adopted a simplified version of the current common distinction of urban and rural based on a population breakpoint of 50,000 served in order to apply it at the county level (Metropolitan Area, 2000; U. S. Census Bureau, 1995b; U.S. Department of Commerce, 1994). That homeless service providers tend to be located in the largest towns of the area they serve suggests the hypothesis that their inception inherently contains an urban element.

I have used the word "transient" in this thesis to describe populations using its basic definition. Although many homeless have been transient, and many locally entrenched among the paupers have historically been encouraged to become transient (either to look for work or through the transference of treatment away from home communities), the homeless hold no claim on the term. In most cases, the term as used in this thesis will refer to all persons not making a place their permanent home, which, in Watauga County, means most of the students attending Appalachian State University as well as many individuals who maintain a primary residence elsewhere.

Research Site

I have lived in Watauga County and worked with its homeless population since 1996. This made the county my first choice as a study area. It was ultimately selected, however, not because it was readily available, but because it is historically a rural county (City-Data.com, 2005; Mance, 2005), and essentially free of the extreme events which have created large and immediate homeless populations in other parts of Appalachia. This combination allows for two things: (1) since the current standard for homeless provision is federally based on the availability of large urban examples, the ready availability of data for Watauga County will allow this and future research to observe and explore variation from the established and inherently biased norm. Such variation becoming available should allow services developing in similar counties to balance their own needs and opportunities as opposed to conforming small community programs to metropolitan practices. (2) The benefit of choosing a county free from large-scale displacements is that this study looks at service provision for the homeless as opposed to looking at homelessness as a factor of disaster response.

Certainly, major events separating people from their homes in Appalachia, such as the Buffalo Creek flood in 1972 (Erikson, 1976) and the Norris Dam relocations in the 1930s (McDonald, 1982), have received much coverage. The trend towards poverty in the region has been observed and scrutinized to the point of creating the Appalachian Regional Commission. However, the everyday causes of Appalachian homelessness and how they have been dealt with have been largely ignored. Scholars have historically wanted everything Appalachian to be relatively homogenous. While focusing primarily on one network of homeless provision centered in Watauga County, North Carolina, this research has looked for similarities throughout Appalachia.

Obviously, working with the homeless professionally prior to beginning this research offers many benefits, including familiarity with, and professional connection to, the local and even regional network, not to mention ready-made informants. The lure of former clients as informants was deemed unreliable. Client objectivity was compromised by the change of roles of their former counselor within a small service provision network. Thus, the IRB filed with the University disallowed the use of service recipients as informants. The preclusion was not restricted to local or previously known recipients, although perhaps it should have been.

Watauga has dealt almost exclusively with day-to-day homelessness. My prior professional experience with the homeless of the county has greatly enhanced my qualitative analysis of the area, despite the fact that it also led me to exclude the homeless themselves from this research's potential range of informants. I have employed a variety of additional methods that include the analysis of archival records, the conducting of interviews with past and present service providers and progenitors, and the administration of a region-wide survey in order to gauge the variety of sufferers among the homeless population and the methods employed towards their return to stability.

Archival Record

Archives were sought in a variety of places, including the existing agencies themselves, libraries, and various county and state archives. The most obvious places to start were within the agencies themselves. Several organizations were able and willing to share internally generated histories. These provided such details as when the agency was formed, who was involved in the formation, and a chronological discussion of major changes in offered programming, as well as insight into how each agency views itself and integrates into the community.

Although I could have expected more college student reports, I knew that they were not usually made available upon completion to libraries or the agencies themselves. Aside from academic involvement in the compilation of the OASIS and Hunger Coalition (Coalition) histories, the only local academic study found was that by Ian Mance, who compiled data from ten years of Hospitality House files (Mance, 2005).

All agencies receiving federal funds turn in statistical reports. Although a shelter survey, discussed subsequently, included a request for such documents, I asked only Hospitality House directly for copies of such data. Consequently, only that agency provided them. Similar data were requested from an American Red Cross shelter in upstate New York during a site visit. Raw data were consistently tracked for all reports at that shelter, allowing pre-official report demographics to be provided.

The Watauga County Courthouse maintains plat maps showing the locations and summary data for all property holdings, including those of relevant agencies and governmental units. The primary utility of those records for this study was the location of the former County Home property, along with when it was surveyed and parceled into marketable lots. The session minutes for Watauga County Commission meetings were accessed for the periods surrounding the opening and closing of the old County Farm. The majority of other pertinent county historical records were either destroyed in courthouse fires (Arthur, 1976) or transferred to the North Carolina State Archives (NCSA) located in Wake County.

The Watauga County records maintained in the NCSA provide several successful bonded bid contracts for several Keepers of the County Home, lists of paupers for a few disparate years, and notes on the condition of the Home from inspections and County Commissioner's reports. Organized counties with an extensive collection of surviving records often listed a variety of relevant data in the catalog available both in text and in microfilm. Unfortunately, Watauga was not one of those counties. Without indexing or other tables of content, much of the microfilmed record appeared to be of such scant and peripheral yield that available time was deemed more efficiently spent elsewhere, especially for the early handwritten years.

The most fruitful records in the State Archives were the Reports of the NC State Board of Public Charities (BoPC) through 1916, the State Board of Charities and Public Welfare (BoC&PW) through 1944, and the State Board of Public Welfare (BoPW) through 1968, being successive reconfigurations of each other. Almost all volumes are on site at the NCSA in Raleigh, and most can be received through the library system if one is patient. Five volumes between 1868 and 1966 are readily available electronically.

State reports fluctuate in the quantity and quality of data presented from year to year regarding the various County Homes and state institutions. Such data often include a description of each County Farm, the capabilities of inmates – mental or physical, the occupancy rate of the Home, who the Keeper and physician were, and how the same were paid. There was also often a prejudicial judgment by the Board as to the quality of the facility and/or its Keeper.

A small variety of texts produced by those Boards, or in evaluation of their efforts, was accessed through the university library system. Similar documents for other Appalachian states were also noted, especially from around New England, but no systematic exploration of them all was pursued. Each state has its own nomenclature where such oversight was concerned, and several began those bodies well before North Carolina. Every volume available for North Carolina was scrutinized. Similar volumes from early New England states were similarly accessed.

Interviews

Five interviews were conducted with directors of various helping agencies in Watauga County. Three additional community members were interviewed. A single director from Tompkins County, New York, was interviewed on two separate visits. Two staff members from an additional Shelter in Washington County, Maryland, were also interviewed. Several agencies in all three locations were visited without interviews.

Although five Appalachian communities outside of Watauga County were originally chosen for site visits, it was determined that such travel was not cost effective to sample during this project. Two members from churches founding Hospitality House were included in the Watauga interviews, as was the Clerk of Court, whose family had been among the last to oversee the County Home when he himself was still a small child. In all, eleven interviews and a handful of conversations were used to further this project.　　The interviews were not uniform in nature, as each was tailored to each respective agency's mission. The data collected filled in gaps left by agency histories when those had previously been made available. Sometimes additional demographics were provided, and almost always descriptions of programs were discussed. When interviewing informants outside of Watauga County, site visits and tours of existing agencies' facilities were also sought. Additionally, I attended a routine meeting of various professionals working within the food pantry system in Ithaca, New York, during a visit in 2008, during which I offered a brief presentation of the Watauga system in exchange for the courtesy.

Surveys

A survey sent out across Appalachia was by far the most cumbersome method of data collection. Many of the addresses found in the initial search proved to be faulty. Many potential contacts were gleaned from various compiled state HUD databases online (Department of Housing and Urban Development, 2006), and a domestic violence shelter list provided by OASIS (Herman, personal communication, March 28, 2006; National Coalition Against, 2004). The majority of the final list came from an internet search of statewide phonebooks (www.whitepages.com, 2006) for each of the Appalachian states. In the five states producing usable returns, there were 185 potential recipients, with a positive response of 19. One of these was faxed with some pages received unclearly. Numerous attempts failed to garner a resend. Thus, the return was roughly 10% of the perceived potential.

As a return envelope was provided, some who received the survey were kind enough to tell me the agency in question had closed or that the business has a name that was misleading. These failed returns were deleted from the original master list. It may be assumed that several such old or otherwise erroneous addresses were simply disposed of upon receipt, but without verification, there is no ready way to identify and delete them from the count. A post-thesis follow up on that particular segment of the project with a simplified survey is expected to produce better results. Several of the positive returns provided up-to-date addresses for shelters in nearby counties, and posting the preliminary data found in this project online should increase both credibility and interest among the technologically connected segment of the expanded list of potential respondents.

Sampling Methodology and Logistics

For the most part, sampling was straightforward. I was generally aiming for 100% representation as close to the original source as could be achieved. With archival data, I had to take what I could find and access in a minimal availability of time. I did not have the luxury of not working full time as a student. The library at Appalachian State University has a wonderful variety of resources available to its students, and a staff that was willing to put some efforts into acquiring less available documents. In the main, there is very little directly pertinent data available specific to Watauga County or the surrounding counties.

As I knew most of my potential informants in Watauga County, I generally went straight to the highest ranked paid staff at any given agency, and was not bashful in talking about my project with agency board members, professors, and local pastors while seeking informants for historic activity. That momentum carried forward when it came to contacting other shelter directors.

The only criteria for survey recipients was that they have a complete address, email, or fax number, and appear to offer shelter services to humans from a location within an Appalachian county. I was appalled to find that there were at least three potential animal shelters for every potential homeless shelter throughout the east coast. After deleting all animal shelters, there were still over 4,000 hits from the thirteen states to be screened. It was with mixed feelings that I watched that number drop to below 400 potential recipients as duplications and non-Appalachian counties were deleted. There were more shelters in some metropolitan cities alone than there were in the entire Appalachian sections of their respective states.

Archive sampling.

When it came to agency specific archive documents, I asked representatives from each agency visited if they had an internally used document and if such was available for my use. In all North Carolina cases where such a document was known to exist it was made available. Additional report data were gleaned from Religious Effort to Assist and Care for the Homeless, Inc. (REACH) in Hagerstown, Maryland, and various agencies in Tompkins County, New York.

Most of the information available through title and deed searches in the Watauga County Court House on current agencies was generally much more efficiently available from the agencies themselves upon request. Various conversations with staff and fellow patrons indicated that qualitative data were absent, and that additional quantitative data were long transferred to the NCSA. Unfortunately, both the Watauga Court House and the NCSA underwent significant renovations during the period when I conducted my research, which made access to some collections difficult or unavailable at times. As with agency histories, if county records existed, I wanted to see them.

In the NCSA, this proved tedious. So little remained from Watauga County records that much was lumped together in the "miscellaneous" file. Because of the courthouse fire, a true continuity of record simply did not remain. What was a whole volume of monthly or quarterly pauper lists and account ledgers in some other counties was only two or three surviving sheets and references scattered throughout the set from Watauga. Data collected in the State Archives included copies of bids and contracts for Keepers of the Poor, reports noted in County Commissioners' minutes, lists of paupers and the corresponding amounts awarded through outdoor relief, as well as recommendations or requests for persons to be considered for inclusion in those same lists.

Since both time and money were severely restricted throughout the process, the non-Watauga Appalachian research conducted at NCSA focused on the quantitative data contained in state reports. Qualitative data for Watauga County were extracted. It was impossible not to notice many biases and lobbied platforms to the General Assembly within those published documents. Analysis of those platforms is not part of this work. For Watauga's part, administrators seemed only to want to be viewed positively. Unfortunately, County Homes became increasingly viewed as substandard to state-run institutions in the early twentieth century, and were progressively treated accordingly in the published record. Homes were ignored completely in some years' reports.

The Board of Public Charities laid a lot of groundwork for future record keeping. Initially the Board sought to collect reports on the status of every County Home, prison, and state institution at least twice a year. The County Home reports included the number of inmates, their capabilities, the location and composition of the Home, the quantity and status of any attached farmed lands, the names of the Keeper and Physician, how they were paid, as well as a rating on the quality of care afforded by the home and/or the Keeper (NCSBoPC, 1870). Appendix B lists the first questions asked of the County Homes. As the Board evolved, much of the thoroughness of the first Board's example was allowed to lapse in favor of new priorities.

During the time overseen by the Board of Charities and Public Welfare (BoC&PW) it was uncommon for individual county reports to be presented to the General Assembly. There was a greater focus on state-maintained institutions by a much more biased board membership. After the Board of Charities and Public Welfare was reformed into the more simply named Board of Public Welfare, data on County Homes remained scant, but became more consistent as the new Board happily counted down which counties had finally taken their advice to become licensed boarding homes for children or the elderly, or had simply closed down altogether, leaving the assorted other facilities to become regional. During that Board's guidance, only Buncombe County, among North Carolina's Appalachian counties, continued to offer a County Home. The variety of services offered early on in Asheville, that county's seat, is discussed more in the chapter on Appalachia. The years around the closure of the Watauga County Home are vague in the state reports, but the Session Minutes of the County Commission are clear that Watauga County succumbed to the pressure to break from the County home model in the late 1940s. The transition covered a period of several years, during part of which the former Home was documented as a boarding home by the state. Despite the change in official purpose, it is doubtful that the inmates noticed a significant change, as even the County Commissioners went about business with little change aside from substituting a lease for the Keeper's contract (Watauga County Registrar, 1960).

Interview sampling.
As previously stated, informants were selected by their connection to the various helping agencies, generally from at or near the top of the salaried staffs. Others were chosen for their connection to an agency at the time of the formation, and asked to speak to the conditions inspiring or impeding formation. All interviewees were met in their own offices with the exception of Father Chuck Blanck. Blanck was unable to make the initial meeting we scheduled at the church he pastors in Alleghany County. While attempting to reschedule, it proved most

efficient to simply go forward with the interview over the phone.

The following, in no particular order, were my informants: Mary Ruth McRae of First Presbyterian Church in Boone, North Carolina; Father Chuck Blanck of Alleghany Christ Church in Sparta, North Carolina, formerly of Saint Luke's Episcopal Church in Boone; Jennifer Herman of OASIS, Inc. in Boone; Glenn Hodges, Watauga County Clerk of Court; Lynne Mason of Hospitality House of Boone, Inc.; Crystal Winebarger of Hunger and Health Coalition in Boone; Marian Peters of Community Cares Clinic in Boone; John Ward of Tompkins County American Red Cross Homeless Services Program in Ithaca, New York; Jim Atkinson of the Department of Social Services in Boone; and, Tina Barse and Jill Parker of REACH, Inc. in Hagerstown, Maryland.

Although not formally interviewed, several individuals provided significant data through more informal meetings. Danielle Harrington of Tompkins Community Action in Ithaca provided data regarding subsidized housing and substance abuse treatment programs in the county. Similarly, Dana Gall described the emergence of a new crisis assistance program offered by the Salvation Army in Watauga County. Although scheduled to meet in her newly christened offices, Gall was establishing the new program in Watauga and Avery Counties concurrently and sought me out at the Northwestern Regional Housing Authority (NRHA) offices where I was performing an unofficial internship at the time.

Almost all of the shorter conversations referenced in this research also took place at the place of employment of the informants, although some occurred in passing at places such as the King Street Post Office, over the phone, or via email. Others aware of either my research or my interest in the subject matter often initiated this more casual networking.

Survey.

The selection of survey recipients has already been outlined above. Email and fax follow-up to those for whom I had found such information triggered an improved rate of response. This indicated that many who did not respond to the original mailing did not actively avoid participation. The same follow-up produced almost all responses apologizing for inability to participate. The survey tool itself is included in Appendix C.

I acquired only eighteen comparable responses, not all of whom answered or demonstrated that they understood every question. Those eighteen came from seventeen different Appalachian counties in five different states: two from Georgia and four each from Tennessee, West

Virginia, Ohio, and North Carolina. In order to increase the accuracy of the findings gleaned from the survey, those surveys that came back undeliverable or acknowledging their impropriety for the survey were stricken from the list, as were surveys sent to states producing no responses. This left 185 potential respondents, and a response rate of just under 10%. Although not ideal, the data gleaned from such a set demonstrates some regional trends and provides updated hypotheses for future study.

With the exception of the North Carolina respondents, there is no discernible connection between myself and the incidence of response. In the case of North Carolina, in addition to several years' work with the homeless providers around Watauga County, I have attended several statewide Emergency Shelter Grant (ESG) conferences from which my name may be recognizable to service providers. Two of the emails and the phone call outlining bad timing were from North Carolina. Surveys were not sent to agencies where interviews and site visits were planned. Since I had so recently left the employ of Hospitality House when I began this project, I had not expected to need an interview with them, and so included them in the mailing. As the scope of this project required more time than anticipated, and word routinely came to me from all sectors that the program's efficacy was suffering, it became obvious that an interview would be useful.

In conjunction with intake forms used at the local shelter, the bulk of survey questions were based on questions asked in the most current Department of Housing and Urban Development (HUD) and Office of Economic Opportunities (OEO) annual report forms as requested from all grant recipients (Department of Housing, 2005; Office of Economic Opportunity, 2005). I had previously used those same reports to update those intake forms at Hospitality House in order to create a tool for initial and final analysis of shelter guests that would allow for easier completion of the most recent versions of those reports. That tool and a description of its creation is included in Appendix D. It was expected that creating the survey in this fashion would facilitate an ease of response among at least those agencies receiving federal funds. It was expected that those receiving other government grants would be tracking similar if not identical data.

The survey as mailed took me twenty-two minutes to fill out using a completed copy of the prior year's annual report to guide my answers.[4] I estimated that the average agency with such reports readily

---

[4] The 2004 as I had filed it used slight variations on essentially the same questions. If I'd had the 2005 reports, which many survey recipients would have been viewing, my time would have

available could complete the survey in approximately thirty minutes. I expected that some agencies would have different tracking demographics and that some of those relying solely on community support would have almost no documentation at all.

Different responders did in fact acknowledge that they did not capture certain types of data. All respondents were polite and professional and expressed a willingness to assist, including several who were unable to supply data because they had either just started their jobs or recently created their agencies. One of the initial intents of the survey was to create an opt-in region-wide database of shelters for the benefit of service providers in Appalachia. The resultant attempt to facilitate partial anonymity of specific types of data created the potential for confusion where anonymity is concerned. For this reason, no tables based solely on individual survey responses are provided in this research. Where discussion of individual responses occur in this thesis, it was clear that such discussion did not breach the trust expected by individual agencies.

Section one of the survey asked for information that was descriptive of the agency. All responses demonstrated an understanding of this section, although in a few instances information was not provided. The section ended with some historical questions regarding when and how the agency was formed. The goals of the section were to identify trends in the creation of services and correct the original mailing list.

Section 2 was a relatively short section that asked the agencies to identify their distinctive programs, who they served, and the nature of their occupation of the properties they utilized. The section ended with questions attempting to discover ownership patterns of program facilities. Such information speaks to what level of trust, dependency, and acceptance an organization interacted within its host community, as well as the level of integration into federal norms regarding homeless service provision.

The next section sought to capture what types of services were being offered. It explored how long shelter was offered versus how long it was being accessed. Such questions should help identify how well the community was addressing potential needs and meeting local needs. Respondents had few problems with this section and varied significantly in their responses. The prevalence of an emergency shelter providing as many non-shelter services as possible was obvious.

The next section surveyed persons served. This was the most difficult section for respondents to provide adequate data. Few responded adequately to all questions and a couple did not respond to this section at

been slightly quicker, as the questions would have been more closely aligned.

all. One shelter offering multiple levels of shelter programming pointed out that the annual reports available applied different age ranges in its computations. It was clear that race and ethnicity are not distinguishable to many providers, despite the fact that governmental censes always differentiate. The goals of this section were to allow comparison and contrast of who needed services in various Appalachian communities.

A final section asked agencies to volunteer information regarding their budgets and if there were other agencies within their region. The goals of this section were to increase the accuracy of the mailing list for a planned follow up to this research, identify levels of governmental support, and gain insight on the size of budgets in relation to staffs. In order to gain a larger response without jeopardizing the response to other sections, the fiscal answers in this section were asked in the form of percentages and ranges.

Inevitably, some problems emerged in the survey administration. The provision of a list of definitions did little to improve the standard usage of terms in question answers. Several questions were less useful for this fact. The term "domestic violence" especially has been such a successfully learned concept that it is seen as an adequate answer to much more specific questions.

A primary obstacle was the fact that the survey was sent out during a time period when many of those agencies for whom it should have been the easiest to complete were in the process of preparing requests for continued funding. Since those grants can currently be garnered for programs with variable grant years different from agency fiscal years, it is impossible not to lose some responses based on such cycles.[5] Since the majority of grants are now offered on a year-to-year basis, it may be timely to incorporate such requests into the end of year annual performance report. When the cycles ran up to three years, it made sense for the request to be held separate.

Methods Conclusion

In my scrutiny of the intersection of homelessness and Appalachia, I have realized several things. Although the directors and

---

[5] While acting as Director of Operations at Hospitality House, I was involved with three such grants, all with different report years, and all different from both the calendar year, the governmental cycle used to acquire local government funds, and the audit cycle required to maintain our right to solicit as a charity. From the beginning of February to the end of July, at least one major report was being compiled, usually requiring overlap adjusted data from at least one of the others. Although this reality was tedious, I cannot imagine that all of them coming due at once would have been easier.

volunteers working in the field are overwhelmingly interested in improving the lives of their clients as well as community understanding of the realities their respective missions address, there is no shortage of tasks to fill their time. Clients and budget are the issues at the top of the list, with everything else claiming time where it can. Which of those two priorities is most important varies by agency and even vacillates within each agency in relation to job descriptions. In fact, they can hardly be separated each from the other in those agencies that have opted into the current nationally supported system; counted clients have become a product for which dollars are paid.

Given this situation, it is easy to see that it will not often be the provider of services who makes the move to get community studies into the hands of the public where those seeking to do regional or even local research can readily access them. Such data are often made available simply upon request, be it to the local reporter, a student pursuing a grade, or a benefactor seeking justification for an investment. When someone else is seeking to make such data available, providers are usually happy to help facilitate those efforts toward expanding the realm of understanding in the community.

Most of the time, little is done with the products of such requests. Most of it simply disappears. Over time, that which remains is stowed away. Much of the data I found useful for this research fell into this category. Government documents and newspaper articles were microfilmed to save space and/or boxed up in archives. Only one of the many research projects I saw undertaken by students while I was providing direct services was provided to the shelter and thus remained available to those undertaking future works.

I have accessed a variety of sources in my quest to compile an overview of homeless service provision in Watauga County. Although it spans over 140 years, it is by no means exhaustive. In drawing comparison to the Appalachian region as a whole, I have looked at reports spanning only about 180 years, but ever since a slave escaped from De Soto's expedition searching for gold in the mid-15th century to be taken in by Cherokee (Davis, 2000), the cultural notions we have of homelessness have been developing.

CHAPTER III

WATAUGA COUNTY HOMELESSNESS

For a variety of reasons, Watauga County is an ideal county for the initial exploration of the Appalachian response to homelessness. Watauga neither excludes nor is excluded by the world around it. Although much of its public records were destroyed in courthouse fires (Arthur, 1976), there is yet some surviving documentation of the provision of services to homeless individuals from as early as 1870, less than 25 years after the county was formed. Watauga currently offers a variety of healthy responses to the issues surrounding homelessness including several agencies that maintain accurate documentation of their histories. Although nothing has been published outside of newspaper articles, a variety of students and journalists routinely observe homelessness issues. Making findings more broadly available is an easy, although seldom taken, next step. Most importantly, Watauga offers examples of the power of community in leading service delivery as well as of the pros and cons of following national trends.

Watauga County is situated in the mountainous region of western North Carolina adjacent to both Tennessee and Virginia. It has experienced many of the changes commonly documented throughout the Appalachian region, such as forest clear-cutting, railway and highway enhancement, the Blue Ridge Parkway, mining, agricultural reform, increasing tourism, recreational and second home development, gentrification, rising property values, and industrial decline. Watauga has also seen its share of flooding, outlaws, and courthouse fires that spice up an otherwise commonplace existence and make the notion of a separate cultural existence more appealing to outsiders.

Conversely, Watauga has not suffered large-scale displacements of individuals on the level of the Tennessee Valley Authority (TVA) relocations in the Norris Dam area of Tennessee (McDonald, 1982), or the Buffalo Creek communities destroyed by a flood of sludge resultant from inappropriate mining practices in West Virginia (Erikson, 1976), and recent relocations related to mountain top coal mining (Reece, 2006). This means that Watauga County's homeless persons became such in common, everyday ways, allowing their stories to be the study of homelessness rather than the study of disaster response.

Figure 2: *Watauga and Appalachian North Carolina.*

Watauga County's total year-round population is approaching 43,000 (Regional Business Services Team, 2005). Appalachian State University accounts for over 15,000 students (Diversity Task Force, 2007) and constitutes the county's largest employer (Regional Business Services Team, 2005). Approximately 13,500 of the year-round residents live in the town of Boone, with the remainder occupying various other towns and the unincorporated portions of the county. "Approximately 18 percent of Watauga County residents live below the poverty level" (Sanders, 2005) despite an apparent unemployment rate of only 3.3% (Regional Business Services Team, 2005).

For many residents of the neighboring counties, Boone is the nearest commercial and employment center. Nearly 3000 people commuted into Watauga for employment in 2000 (Regional Business Services Team, 2005). Thus, Boone is also a regional urban center. In addition to the labor attracting properties of Boone, Watauga's highways facilitate employment transit from neighboring counties in Tennessee to Caldwell and Wilkes Counties to the south and east of Watauga respectively. The confluence of several highways in Boone allows it to capture a large percentage of seasonal travelers, while temperate climate and proximity to seasonal recreation cause many of those to become transient residents of the region.

Early Homelessness in the County

The earliest references found related to helping the homeless in Watauga County regard the County Home system. In 1870, state record indicates that Watauga had no County Home, but was spending $300 a year on the upkeep of eight paupers living in private homes (NCSBoPC, 1870). Despite the lapse in published Board reports, old County records show that in 1876 a Mr. Thomas Hagaman was awarded a bonded bid contract to keep 14 individuals of mixed gender and surname for a period of one year starting in October of that same year (Hagaman & Critcher, 1876). The contract is not as specific as in later years, so it is not clear if Hagaman was acting as the Keeper of a county facility or using his own properties. Regardless, a formal contract demonstrating responsibility beyond that of outdoor relief had been introduced. The presence of a bond secured on that contract makes it clear that the arrangement was more than the standard upkeep of a few relatives or neighbors falling on hard times.

In 1882, the county purchased 130 acres of what became known as the County Home Property for $1000 (Councill & Hayes, 1882). Since county and state records reported various acreages over the years for the size of the property, this does not actually substantiate or deny the possibility that Hagaman was Keeper of a County-owned Home, but it does mark an official beginning of the County's commitment to the contemporary norm of offering shelter associated with a farm contributing to its own upkeep, i.e. the adoption of the county home model.

By 1887, there were reports on the condition of the county facilities (jail, Home, and courthouse) beginning to show up in records of the County Commission. Although short, such comments as "A committee of three visited the poor house and found that the buildings are in good condition. The paupers are well cared for." (Watauga County Commission, 1887) demonstrated the key components of County protocol. It was desired that the Home be maintained and that the residents of the same were given adequate provision.

Although the County Home was often only given a couple of lines stating that the inmates and grounds were adequately cared for, contracts for successful bids often included instructions on various maintenance upgrades to be made (Watauga County Deeds, 1931) and reports to the State Board often expressed pride in the care given by overseers. W.B. Councill, Watauga Superintendant of Health and default

Table 3.1 *Early Population of the Watauga County Home*

	Inmate Populations of the Home				Outdoor Relief
	Adult		Child		
	White	Colored/Black	White	Colored/Black	
1892	7, 9				10
1893	6				10-Aug
1894	7				10
1895	7				10-Aug
1896	7				10-Jun
1897	9, 8				10-Jun
1898	8				10
1899	-				-
1900	9				-
1901	5	1			31
1902	5	0			-
1903	7		2		41
1905	8	2	1°		40
1908	9	1	1 blind		40
1909	10, 13±	1	1,0		40
1910	13, 14, 15±	0, 1±			40
1911	13, 14				35
1912	13			1	40
1913	6				40
1914	15			1	
1915	8			-	
1916	7			2	40

°Child sent to orphanage

±3 the final number in these cells were provided by a statistical summary provided in addition to the presented county reports

Sources: North Carolina State Board of Public Charities, publication year is the year after report year noted in the table.

physician for all formal County residential facilities, especially seemed proud of the County's work during the later years of the nineteenth century. At the end of one report he remarked that, "The people of Watauga County feel justly proud of their home for the poor and feel it their privilege to keep the inmates as neat, comfortable and happy as possible" (NCSBoPC, 1894, p. 75).

The 1890s saw the numbers of individuals sheltered by the home hover between 7-10 inmates while 6-10 received "outdoor aid" (NCSBoPC, 1892, 1894, 1896, 1898, 1901). Outdoor signified general financial aid provided outside the County Home. Such relief was usually a monthly-valued stipend paid quarterly to a designated friend or family member to help with essentials. It was also often extended as credit or goods instead of cash (G. Hodges, personal communication, March 7, 2006). After 1900, the number receiving outdoor relief rose dramatically, reaching 40 individuals by 1905, although the residency rate at the home remained at 10 or less (NCSBoPC, 1901, 1902, 1904, 1905, 1906, 1908, 1910, …). The sheltered population climbed as high as 15 by 1911 (NCSBoPC, 1912) after which levels dropped considerably as pressures to remove those with mental obstacles (including epilepsy) especially, and orphans secondarily, to specialized state or regionally run facilities continued to increase (NCSBoPC, 1912). Outdoor relief remained constant at least through 1916, when the recasting of the State Board of Public Charities halted the routine presentment of statistical summaries (NCSBoC&PW, 1918).

Table 3.1 compiles the census data presented by the North Carolina State Board of Public Charities to the General Assembly covering the years 1868 - 1916. After the initial report filed in 1870, when there was yet no Home in Watauga County, no reports were filed for a number of years due to a lack of budget. Although it seldom happened in early years, Watauga County sometimes failed to submit its reports. The Board compiled reports submitted by each county twice a year, in either spring or summer and then again in fall or winter. As population numbers were generally stable, counties often did not file or simply stated that there was no change, transferring the burden of transcribing or estimating details onto the members of the Board. Occasionally, the state conducted surveys that added details from a third time period. Such surveys are early parallels to the Point-in-Time Surveys we now compile yearly to estimate actual statewide need.

From Table 3.1, it is immediately clear that declaration of race was not always included in Watauga's report, especially where children are concerned. After 1911, existing reports indicate only Whites when they specify race at all, a trend that continues through 1939, after which few clear statistics are found for the Home. When more than one number is included under inmate populations, reports filed during the year demonstrated a change in population, except where additional notes are provided. In all other years, there was either no change, or there was only one report. A notation such as "6-10" represents the submission of the compiler of the report to the state, and is assumed to represent monthly fluctuation during the six months reported upon.

One exception should be noted. The 1910 biennial report included a statistical chart of all counties. The statistical analysis was completed for yet a third set of data. The final number of inmates shown represents the population as determined on that third date. Those who received outdoor aid may have lived in homes they owned, or may have lived in the home of family or neighbors.

By 1908, and possibly as early as 1905, the child represented as part time was a blind girl who spent part of her educational years in a state school for the blind. She returned home at least for the summer (NCSBoPC, 1911). It is possible that she is the same blind woman who shows up in the 1915 report (NCSBoPC, 1916). If this is true, despite the specialized state care, her handicap still prevented her from reintegrating into society.

The year 1922 marks the only documentation found for outdoor relief in Watauga County after the North Carolina Board of Public Charities became the Board of Charities and Public Welfare. At that time, there were only 20 individuals receiving such aid (NCSBoC&PW, 1922), down to half of the long time figure reported by the county to the state. It is possible that this is partially due to population and opportunity shifts brought about by the end of World War I. The decline is certainly attributable in part to the rise in more preventative types of assistance, such as Mothers' Aid, which targeted select populations in their own homes.

As has already been stated, the rise in preventive measures also came with a reduction of clear documentation of who was and was not homeless. From the County Commission Meeting Docket, we can tell that Watauga still doled out assistance from the General Fund at least as late as the mid-1950s, when the County Home property was parceled and sold (Watauga County Registrar, 1960).

Throughout the early and mid twentieth century, County records indicate that there was a strong practice of County coffers being used like a bank for orphans, with deposits from estates and any other sources being held and doled out to guardians until the youth were old enough to claim the balance (NC Clerk of Superior Court, 1969; NC Dept. of Archives and History, 1969).

During the 1930s, as with the rest of the country, many changes were coming about in the area of community aid. Watauga's County Home was still going strong, even though many counties in the nation were taking the opportunity to consolidate into regional shelters or simply fade away. The State of North Carolina was strongly pushing for such consolidations to occur. Wade Edward Brown, later to be the county's attorney, was becoming actively involved in the politics of the Watauga community. By the middle of the decade, he had helped to establish a chamber of commerce, secured a county agent position for the local farmers, and became the local advocate for the Home Owner's Loan Corporation (HOLC) program, assisting with home loans for those same farmers, securing 35 loans to keep farmers from losing their land (Brown, 1997).

Throughout North Carolina, though primarily in the Piedmont region, the state had been promoting various relocation community projects that aimed to teach landowners how to make a living from their own new small farms (Cutter, 1935). The plan was ultimately perceived as poorly executed, but home loans to existing farmers trying to keep family land was proving to be a bit more effective. Eventually, the HOLC program was opened up to non-farm homeowners as well (Brown, 1997).

The 1930s also saw the beginning of what would become the Blue Ridge Parkway. Governmental need to minimize the overall expense for taxpayers meant that many of the local landowners, including a number of farmers, were paid less for land that was seized than they had paid for it years before. The designation of "scenic byway" meant that access was legally restricted to those pursuing recreational purposes. Farmers who lived along the route were not able to access the road to further their trade.

Livelihood was further threatened if a road previously depended upon for transporting farm products had been destroyed or left on the opposite side of the Parkway from dependent farms; many were effectively prohibited from continuing their previous work. Easements prevented many activities or forced property improvements that residents could not afford. Since the various governments were not interested in buying extra-easement properties, holding or selling unworkable properties for some uncertain use was the only legal option for many (Whisnant, 2006). Brown himself bought up several properties in the area (Brown, 1997).

In counterpoint, as environmental demands on farmable land combined with other community pressures to render subsistence methods of livelihood less effective, many struggling individuals and families were introduced to the short-term benefits of wage labor as the Blue Ridge Parkway and various New Deal/WPA projects, including the Downtown Boone Post Office (High Country Back Roads, 2006), provided temporary jobs in the county.[6] Some were able to increase the scope of their social networks and their resume of marketable skills, thereby opening means to previously unknown or inaccessible opportunities.

Glenn Hodges (personal communication, 2006), Watauga County Clerk of Court, recalls that his family kept the County Home for several years until 1941, at which time he was still a very small child. He recalls, partly from information passed on by his elders, that during his time on the farm, the facility consistently sheltered between 10 and 20 individuals, usually unable to assist on the farm but generally cooperative with their hosts. Electricity had only recently come to that part of the county, an event that greatly helped his mother and one paid assistant with household chores.

The produce of the farm, although partially used on site, according to Hodges, was primarily sold to truckers who congregated in an ad hoc farmers' market along the highway in Boone for the purpose of buying from the local farmers who came to promote their various products. Once an agreement was reached, the trucker would travel to one or more farms to collect his purchases. The reports presented in the state annuals, and the details provided by contracts preserved in archived county records suggest that this was a long time practice. Those records also corroborate with Hodges that the stipend received by the Keeper was augmented by any profits that could be gleaned from the farm itself. Timbering was prohibited unless requested by the County Commission, and then limited amounts were approved for fence repair or to open up additional tracts for cultivation or grazing purposes. (See Appendix E for some transcribed contracts.) Hodges is further aware that another family

---

[6] Although Boone's Downtown Post Office was constructed as a WPA project, it is commonly misconceived that the 1940 mural it contains was also contracted by the WPA. Alan Tompkins' well known "Daniel Boone on a hunting trip in Watauga County" was actually contracted by the U.S. Treasury Department (Eason, 2007; Lorance, 2006).

operated the farm after his moved. He believes that the farm was unoccupied for a few years before most of it sold. The home itself was rededicated as the county's first rest home.

County Commission minutes confirm that J. R. Simmons was the Keeper through December 1942; then Grady Hayes took over in January 1943 as the last Keeper under the traditional model. The re-routing of Highway 421 in early 1945 provided the local catalyst for the decline of the service. The new highway separated four acres from the County Home property, which were subsequently listed for sale (Watauga County Registrar, 1960; Winkler, 1945). Unlike the farms bisected by the Blue Ridge Parkway, the County Home was located on a commercial road where livelihoods could still be pursued from such a parcel.

By October of 1945 same year, the Home was closed, and the inmates were officially placed under the care of the Superintendent of Welfare, David Mast, and directed to be placed in boarding homes. Hayes remained as Keeper during the transition, and was even reconfirmed as such in February 1946. The use of the Home itself as a boarding house was at least being explored during that summer.

Hayes ultimately signed a lease on the property in November, marking the end of the County home model in Watauga and the local beginning of the regional boarding home model. Although official reports on the home become less frequent, the County Commission does not seem to recognize any change in their responsibilities. Session minutes do not acknowledge the distinction until the term "County Boarding Home" shows up in October 1948 (Watauga County Registrar, 1960).

Watauga County may not have recognized a change in operations, but the state appeared satisfied. The 1948 Biennial Report was able to show a reduction from 64 to 59 remaining County Homes in North Carolina, two of which became Boarding Homes while three counties made multicounty agreements for indigent care (NCSBoPW, 1948a). Since the five counties closing their homes were not identified, another report published by the state the same year is needed to confirm that Watauga was one of them. A tabulation of County Home residency in NC was published too late to offer data relevant to this study beyond the fact that Watauga County no longer had a Home for the Aged and Infirm in July, 1946 (NCSBoPW, 1948b). North Carolina lists the licensing of a boarding home in Watauga County by Mrs. Grady Hayes during its 1947 fiscal year. The Home was capable of housing up to 39

White individuals. Although several other boarding homes existed in Appalachia at the time, the only two listed for Blacks were in Winston-Salem and Asheville (NCSBoPW, 1948a). Both of those cities were long common locations for state-run regional facilities.

Although the inmates are routinely cited as being well cared for under Hayes, the Home itself was perpetually in need of significant repairs. The lease was granted to Lee Combs in 1949, followed by Thomas Miller in 1951. During this time, the Commission was clearly divided in its desires for the property. The decision was made in May 1950 to sell, only to be rescinded in July. Even though an inventory of the Home at the time of Miller's occupation proved furnishings to be so dilapidated as to be almost worthless, a fire escape was added in April, 1951. There is no residential description of the property after June of the same year, when the town of Boone was granted a one-year right-of-way for dumping waste along the Old Road Way located on the County Home Property (Watauga County Registrar, 1960).

Throughout the period after Hodges and his family vacated the Home, various notations related to general care payments, ranging from one-time grocery assistance up to four months on poor relief roles, appear throughout the session minutes. These are interspersed with directions to pay for responsibilities incurred to regional facilities including Black Mountain Sanitarium and Banner Elk Orphanage, demonstrating that Watauga County was complying on some level with the state's ideas of regional care. A summary of boarding home residency disclosed that persons were accepted into the Watauga County Boarding Home from throughout the region (Watauga County Registrar, 1960).

Most of the property was surveyed, parceled and sold by the county, the work being overseen by previously mentioned attorney Brown, between January and September 1955 (Watauga County Registrar, 1960; Watauga County Registrar of Deeds, 1955). Part of the property remains in the county holdings today having afforded aid to one of the first Boarding Homes in the County, followed by the first Health Department, built in 1955 at the corner of what is now the Hwy 105 bypass and Hwy 421. The Health Department building eventually became the adult education center for the Watauga Campus of Caldwell Community College and Technical Institute (CCC&TI) when it relocated to a location off Bamboo Road. The building now sits vacant as future uses are unhurriedly debated (R. Nelson, personal communication, March, 2008). Unfortunately, Brown did not mention the Home or its sale in his memoire.

Grady Woodring (personal communication, 2008), a former truck driver who has lived his entire life in the area, recalls that a man named Tommy Roark was living in the boiler room of Watauga's Court House in the late 1940s. The arrangement appeared to be that he was in charge of keeping up the building, although it is unclear if the arrangement was official or incidental in nature. It is also unknown if others squatted or frequented local government buildings for temporary shelter. The Court House was routinely used by the public for a variety of functions in accordance with a standard fee schedule to ensure that the room could be kept lighted, heated, cleaned and orderly for such purposes. The County Commission hired a couple in September 1955 to make janitorial and security measures more consistent. The couple was to oversee the buildings and grounds of the Court House, County Building, and Jail, including making sure doors were locked after staff had exited, no later than 5:30 pm (Watauga County Registrar, 1960).

Beginnings of the Current Services

After July 1951, no record is found of any local activity clearly relatable to homeless assistance until, in the 1960s, Community Action Agencies (CAAs) began to be formed nation-wide. During that time, those without shelter were left to find help where they could, which included abandoned barns, open churches, and their automobiles if they had them (C. Blanck, personal communication, March 29, 2006; Mance, 2005). Although Community Action Agencies did not focus on homelessness, their actions usually went a long way towards minimizing the occurrence, and many CAAs became the first housing authorities nationwide.

WAMY Community Action (WAMY) was locally formed in 1964 with the mission "to provide aid in correcting and eliminating conditions which result in the economic, social, and physical handicaps present among low income individuals in the North Carolina counties of Watauga County, Avery, Mitchell and Yancey" (Norris, 2007). WAMY developed out of the efforts of the North Carolina Fund, begun by Governor Sanford through the private sector in 1963, as one of its first eleven funded agencies (Angela Miller, personal communication, Summer, 2008). The Office of Economic Opportunity (OEO) adopted the concept the following year, pursuant to the national Economic Opportunity Act (Cerese & Channing, 2008). Thus, it began before the nation decided to promote the idea. Sadly, even the North Carolina Fund would become dependent primarily on federal funding through OEO during its planned five-year lifespan (Cerese & Channing, 2008).

Although the Department of Housing and Urban Development (HUD) began work in the 1960s, Northwestern Regional Housing Authority (NRHA), the local housing authority, was not up and running until 1976, according to Ned Fowler (personal communication, April 14, 2006). Fowler, the key player in starting NRHA, has been the Director of the agency since that time.

An interview with Father Chuck Blanck (personal communication, March 29, 2006), who moved to Boone in 1975 as the Pastor of St. Luke's Episcopal Church informs that local churches frequently left their doors unlocked up until that time to allow those who needed to come in at night a reasonably safe place to do so. An increasing population in the town was leaving churches more often victims of vandalism, and as of the time of Father Blanck's arrival, St. Luke's alone routinely left its doors open year round. Although Blanck recalls that he and his church were generally well cared for, casual talks with other town pastors, while I was a shelter director, indicate that vandalism and embarrassing clean-ups had led to various church administrative decisions to begin locking their doors. This went against a commonly held perception among many of the clergy and congregation that locking various church doors went against the duty of the Church. On the coldest nights, the last to leave was often a bit forgetful in regards to certain doors.

In my interview with Father Blanck, I learned that around the time that he arrived in Watauga County, the Methodist, Episcopalian, and Catholic Community Association (MECCA)[7] was beginning a mission to provide aid whenever it could. It was delivering meals once or twice a week, and making small loans to the impoverished in Junaluska, the local Black community. This group of three downtown churches eventually was joined by the Baptist and Lutheran churches and became known as the Downtown Coalition of Churches.[8] The observation that St. Luke's unofficial overnight census in the late-1970s was reaching as

---

[7] A $10,000 check from a northern Islam group unfortunately had to be returned when it was verified that the acronym had caused some confusion.

[8] Those six churches were St. Luke's Episcopal, St. Elizabeth's Catholic, Boone United Methodist, Grace Lutheran, First Presbyterian, and First Baptist. The first three have since moved from their former locations. Although First Baptist is the only church currently in the official downtown district, most of the others are only blocks away.

high as 17 or 18 people, often from out of town, alerted the group that it was becoming time for an actual shelter that could offer supervision and case management.

About the same time, the local mental health agency was directed to begin providing services for victims of domestic violence and rape. The resultant community meetings attracted the positive attentions of a variety of people including representatives from the local school systems, Appalachian State University's Psychology and Social Work programs, and the local Department of Social Services. In very short order, Opposing Abuse with Service, Information and Shelter (OASIS) was formed and began offering services to victims in Watauga and Avery counties. The new agency quickly formulated and subsequently realized its goal to operate independently of the other involved organizations by pursuing its own status as a 501©3 charitable institution in 1978 (Star-Stilling, 1998).

Short-term emergency shelter for those fleeing domestic violence situations was arranged through discounted rates offered by Boone Trail Motel or via transportation to shelters in nearby Caldwell or Wilkes counties. Apartments were occasionally rented while it was possible for the victim and program names to be withheld from databases and other inquiry from estranged partners and potential stalkers. In 1981, the local Unitarian Universalist Fellowship Hall was able to offer the first stable shelter. The total operating budget for the organization that year was only $4000. By 1982, a 24-hour crisis line was operational and the first paid staff member, Libby Detter, was hired (Herman, personal communication, 2006; Star-Stilling, 1998).

The Coalition of Churches also recognized an increased potential for women seeking aid to become victims of abuse under the prevailing system and made similar arrangements with area hotels, although not always with acceptable results. Blanck recalled cases in both extremes of that early situation. In one case, multiple women had been put up in a hotel, only to turn out to be using the rooms for prostitution. In another case, a woman had fled to Boone from an abusive situation. After staying a time and composing herself, she found a quieter life as the caretaker of a local elderly woman.

In the midst of this time, the Watauga County Hunger Coalition also had its beginnings. Joan Chater's two young sons decided they wanted to throw a Christmas party in 1980 to collect food and diapers for the region's less fortunate. The area's faith groups had found that they were increasingly getting requests for food assistance. Subsequent conversations led the Boone United Methodist Church to offer an empty closet to be used as a collection and distribution space, seeded with those original party donations (Hunger Coalition Staff, 2005).

Closet space was quickly outgrown as the idea caught on. By the end of the first year, the pantry had moved into a space located above Legal Services of the Blue Ridge. Members of the Watauga Chapter of United Way helped the fledgling agency draw up a board of directors and articles of incorporation, which were approved in January 1982. In 1984, the Coalition moved again to Hardin Street, to the site now occupied by the Footsloggers' climbing tower, and hired their first paid director. The chaotic nature of the business caused the new administrator to resign after only 6 months. Cinda McGuinn was hired and quickly joined forces with the Second Harvest Food Bank. She also strengthened ties with the local faith community to create the Faith Community Fund, which sought to financially help those in danger of a variety of crises, including immanent eviction or electric cut-off. McGuinn directed the agency for the next twelve years (Hunger Coalition Staff, 2005).

The official opening of a general shelter for the homeless was a bit longer in coming. According to Father Blanck's pocket planners, weekly meetings began in October of 1984 over breakfast every Friday at 7:15 am at the Holiday Inn. The first offer on a facility was a house for sale in a nice neighborhood. The purchase was offered by "a friend in Florida" in response to a newspaper advertisement. Unfortunately, one of the prospective neighbors was a bank president who took offense to the idea of a shelter in his neighborhood. Together with a local lawyer, the pursuit of the opportunity was blocked until a ninety-day window imposed on the sale had elapsed. The woman who was going to buy the house was fortunately able to get her money back from the seller (M. R. McRae, personal communication, March 7, 2006).

Connie Humphreys offered the current location of "Hospitality House" for donation after the college fraternity that inhabited the building threw a party that left the house a shambles, closed King Street, and overflowed into the parking lot of nearby First Baptist Church (McRae, 2006). Both Mary Ruth McRae and Father Blanck stated that various local churches and civic groups each chipped in by "adopting" and repairing a room. An anonymous donor made a generous donation to get the organization going, although Father Blank recalls that there was a perpetual problem with financing the budget through 1996, when he left Boone. Since I began working with the local homeless about the same time as Blanck left, I can attest that, although that particular problem never truly abated, things had a way of working out.

    That location was not without its detractors, to be sure. Mary Ruth McRae recalls that some seasonal members of the First Presbyterian Church congregation were upset that a shelter was going up within sight of the church. One such member called the pastor at the time to complain. The pastor ultimately had to point out directly to the member that such views were not in line with Christian teaching and therefore did not supersede the Church's involvement in promoting the mission.

    The charter creating Hospitality House of the Boone Area, Inc. was hand delivered to Raleigh late in 1984 (Blank, 2006), much as Wade Brown had found it expeditious to hand deliver the papers necessary to begin offering farm loans to the state capitol for endorsement fifty years earlier (Brown, 1997). In February of 1985, the shelter opened for business. In 1986, the shelter began offering a soup kitchen sponsored by area churches called the Bread of Life Meal Program. During the following two years, the shelter refined its services to ensure safety and comfort for the majority of its presenting guests (Hospitality House Shelter Staff, 2005).

    The basement of Hospitality House was offered as sleeping accommodation in the winter for street people and those with addictions, such as alcoholism, that prevented them from maintaining stable housing or successfully following shelter requirements year round. In the winter of 1988/9, with assistance from the Interagency Council, a Homelessness Task Force, and the Coalition of Churches, a plan was created to once again have the downtown churches host the winter crowd in monthly rotation, beginning at nearby First Baptist Church. Unfortunately, rotation proved unwieldy and "The Sleeping Place" remained at First Baptist Church until a relocation committee was able to secure the former Hagaman Clinic on downtown King Street for the winter of 1991 (Hospitality House, 2005).

    Father Blanck recalls that the only death occurring on shelter related property during his time in Boone occurred during one of those early attempts at winter shelter. The body of a man known to frequently stay in the shelter was found in an alleyway outside one of the helping churches. The man is believed to have died as a result of his habit of consuming alcohol collected from such sources as hair spray and mouth wash. It is quite possible that this event was an impetus for pursuing the former Hagaman Clinic as a stable winter shelter, where better-trained supervision could be achieved. There would not be another death of a sheltered guest until after the 2002 creation of Rock Haven, a permanent assisted living program opened by Hospitality House, allowed clients with greater health needs to be served long-term.

While Hospitality House was sorting out winter woes during its early years, OASIS was creating needed support programming for its guests, educational programming for the community, building its staff and, in the summer of 1988, acquiring its first house with the help of the Janirve and Z. Smith Reynolds Foundations (Starr-Stilling, 1998). The new home would stabilize shelter for many of those presenting at the OASIS offices.

The year 1989 was one of change for the Hunger Coalition. A bar and grille was offered the space they had been using, and the Coalition was told it had a month to find a new home. They moved to a location on King Street, directly across from the Court House. Although that move was chaotic, the same year saw them begin offering a free clinic through the Health Department, their first annual Thanksgiving Community Dinner, and the very popular Sharing Tree, which ensures that Santa Claus will not miss local less fortunate children (Hunger Coalition Staff, 2005).

In 1990, the first stable Director of Hospitality House was hired. Under the leadership of Rev. Jim Thompson, and with guidance by NRHA, the facility became in 1992 one of the first recipients in the state of a transitional shelter grant offered through HUD. Transitional shelter could offer a longer and more comprehensive stay for clients with greater needs. Some of the programs offered under the new grant included various options for childcare and on-site GED classes. Thompson would compassionately direct the shelter from 1990 until he was retired in 2005. In a similar stroke of good fortune, Jennifer Herman became the Executive Director of OASIS in the winter of 1991 and remains the director to this day.

In February of 1995, Chater and another Coalition volunteer, Doug McCloughlin, began a free pharmacy program. McCloughlin also quickly started the Warm Hearth Program with the help of students in Watauga High School's Mountain Alliance Program. Firewood was collected, chopped, and made available to those trying to stay warm over the winter. In January of 1996, Ceia Webb took over as the Coalition's Director, and the Pharmacy Program became the nation's first to take to the streets. Renamed the Country Roads Mobile Pharmacy, the program was able to offer greater access for its beneficiaries in Watauga County, Ashe, Avery, and even Alleghany Counties (Hunger Coalition Staff,

2005).

In the summer of 1996, I joined the staff of Hospitality House of Boone as a work-study student. The shelter had three buildings. Two facilities were operating from the original property location at 302 West King Street. The third facility was a five-minute walk up the road towards downtown at 492 West King Street.

The main shelter included two partially separated staff offices, a room for an overnight manager, a living room, the kitchen, and six bedrooms, five of which were upstairs. Excluding staff presence, the shelter could house up to 22 people and was usually close to full. It offered an evening meal to all comers, usually about 35 people, served by a different church, civic group, or business each night. Breakfast and lunch were available to those receiving shelter, usually on a serve yourself from what you can find basis, although someone would frequently step forward to turn the random contributions into a more orderly meal or buffet. The shelter took full advantage of the USDA's food redistribution program and sporadic advantage as a member of the Second Harvest Food Bank of Northwest North Carolina. At an unclear point in the home's first few years, the long front porch had been enclosed, which provided expansions to both office space and the communal living room.

The small house behind the primary facility, commonly known as "The Rock House" or more formally as "The Rock Annex," was persistently troublesome to lend purpose. Most of my time employed it was rented through HUD's Section 8 program[9] as one of very few houses in town that could support a large family. It offered four bedrooms, 2-1/2 baths, a kitchen, a living room, a large backyard, and a full basement with laundry facilities. Its proximity to the primary homeless shelter led to some interesting times for the staff as dual programs meant that guidelines and responsibilities often had to be re-explained to residents of each, as well as to a constant flow of largely inexperienced volunteers – mostly short-term ones from the university across the street.

The desire for a separate general shelter for women was lauded regularly for the Rock Annex, but the tendency for homeless women to also be fleeing domestic violence situations meant they were frequently a

---

[9] Section 8 is officially named the Housing Choice Voucher Program, and offers income based rental assistance to qualified applicants in qualified community properties. Waiting lists in cities are often quite large and take months to rotate. The same program can operate low-cost complexes, including those frequently known as "the projects."

high-risk minority among our clientele. Many of them were helped successfully through OASIS's programs, including most of those capable of operating with minimal supervision. Too often, we did not have enough women at one time who were ready for the reduced supervision offered, or the women we did have had children too old to stay in such a small room with a parent. A couple years before I became the Operations Director in 2002, the shelter became a transitional facility for four to five individuals with longer-term needs and a demonstrated lack of need for on-site supervision. The home is still able to receive Section 8 funds administered by Northwestern Regional Housing Authority. The shelter afforded an unofficial Rock Annex preference to women entering the transitional program, while families were considered accordingly for The Sleeping Place, where too many single individuals would face increased temptations of nearby bars.

The downtown facility originally had shared a building with a take-out pizza place but had eventually been purchased in its entirety. It still enjoyed a duality of purpose as one half served the winter crowd half the year (sometimes all year) and the other side served an additional four transitional guests year round. The building was essentially divided on the diagonal, with the southwest side serving wintertime guests with one large dorm room for men, one small one for women, one full and two half baths, a living room with a kitchenette, and a very small room where an overnight volunteer could sleep just inside a closed in porch.

The full bath, with the only shower, operated in accord with whoever got to it first. The men's dorm had ten bunks, and the women's had five. Three couches and several extra hand-me-down[10] prison mattresses allowed extra space when needed. An enclosed front porch, an addition to the original structure, offered a sitting place for smokers without the need to go outside in the cold winter weather, along with a deterrent to temptations provided by the nearby bars that leaving supervision to smoke outside would afford. Being outside the original brick wall, the room offered little protection from the cold. During most of the winter, the 15 beds were enough, but I have seen nights when over 30 people were seeking the shelter's aid. The 2000/2001 winter saw 121 different people make use of that shelter, but roughly half only stayed a

---

[10] Many of the mattresses and beds came directly from the prison when it closed. A camp that had received some of the beds eventually closed itself, and offered the shelter the opportunity to acquire some of their beds when attrition made it opportune. Unfortunately, most of their beds had faired as badly. Hearts of Hospitality, an auxiliary fund-raising group to the Hospitality House Board, eventually bought all new beds.

night or two. Many of those were helped with gas vouchers, motel stays, & car repairs through Mann Travelers' Aid funds, which were administered by Hospitality House to prevent travelers from becoming stranded en route through the area.

The northeast half of the building served four transitional guests with two small bathrooms, a large living room, and a large kitchen, as well as both entrances to the medium sized parking area behind the building. The parking area was frequently used as overflow parking for guests of the emergency shelter.[11] In the summer time, the winter shelter quarters were used to expand the transitional program for families who appeared in control enough to achieve stable housing before wintertime returned.

The Sleeping Place's nearest neighbors were a restaurant to the west, a bar and grille across the street to the south, an inaccessible apartment building up a steep bank to the north, and a vacant wooded lot up a steep bank to the east. The bar across the street offered several apartments upstairs that were popular with alcohol-minded college students. Where the bar's influence on certain of our clients was easily foreseeable, the apartments provided interesting scenarios at random intervals that kept staff on its toes and shaking its head. The beat cops patrolling the area were occasionally asked to casually let tenants of those apartments know the nature of the facility on occasions when alcohol and loose clothing led students to provide inappropriate shows to shelter guests.

The vacant lot was affectionately referred to as "Sherwood Forest" by those in the know and provided frequent camping spots off and on for those ineligible, usually by personal life choices, for the beds offered by the local shelter system, as well as to town drunks who were simply too besotted to make it home. The lot was roughly accessible from the north and easily accessible from the street to the south. It would not be until around 2004 that regular police patrols virtually eliminated the allure of the site for a centralized campsite.

In my first years at the shelter, I did not work directly with client cases or statistics. My duties centered around the food programs and ensuring that the house stayed stocked on basic supplies. Although my

---

[11] Parking was a persistent problem at the emergency shelter. Although most of the sheltered guests no longer had vehicles, guests and volunteers of the soup kitchen often used space at the Bingham House, which shared the driveway, and the First Baptist Church lot across the street as overflow. Understanding varied over time, depending on neighbor relations, church functions, and church administrators.

interactions with clients were the casual guidance in getting their chores done, and finding items like soap and towels, I know that we were citing the average length of stay in emergency shelter as 17 days. The Rock Annex was then being rented through NRHA to large families, and the Sleeping Place had only a small number of transitional guests. In some summers, a few of the more chronic and disabled winter shelter guests would stay year round. I do not recall any demographics kept specific to that group. Beginning in the winter of 1998, I was asked to help upgrade that section of the program under the supervision of Robert Cox, who was the Associate Director through early 2002.

In 1998, the United Way of Watauga County expanded its services to neighboring Ashe and Avery Counties, becoming the High Country United Way. The Watauga County Hunger Coalition followed suit with its mobile pharmacy travelling even as far as Alleghany County. They officially shortened their name to Hunger Coalition. Yet another move for the Coalition was precipitated by another incoming restaurant, and this time the Coalition would move to 417 Meadowview Road, also in Boone, its fifth and last forced move (Hunger Coalition Staff, 2005).

By 1999, it was becoming more and more common for Coalition patrons to be suffering either from disabling conditions that made food preparation difficult, or from a lack of kitchen facilities. The Food Recovery Program took advantage of the Good Samaritan laws and began gleaning excess food from area restaurants to prepare and distribute to those in need, greatly expanding the Coalition's ability to help. The growing need for prescription aid for medications the Coalition was not allowed to distribute or could not keep in stock also triggered the start of the Individual Drug Program. This program essentially helps those who qualify for assistance with the paperwork and verification necessary to have certain medications delivered directly from the provider to the recipients' door much more cheaply than from the pharmacy (Hunger Coalition Staff, 2005).

Meanwhile, OASIS was undergoing different stresses. They had been benefiting from free office space in First Baptist Church for a number of years. This allowed the location of their shelters to maintain a high level of anonymity, their prospective clients to maintain a level of ambiguity of visible purpose when dropping in for a chat, and the agency itself to enjoy the existence of a small but growing reserve in its savings account – a luxury that most non-profits in the area never get to enjoy.

The induction of a new pastor allowed a brief administrative disconnect from the church's local philanthropy and the OASIS staff began to feel that their location had become more tenuous.[12] They began looking at options. Although the situation soon settled, the idea of a permanent dedicated building offering a better arrangement of space to a growing staff and new programming led the agency to turn its modest fiscal reserves into a down payment on a house on Meadowview Drive, next door to the Hunger Coalition. The move maintained most of the benefits the church space had provided while offering several new opportunities. Since property values were by then escalating rapidly, there would also be a guaranteed return on their investment when they decided to sell.

The Hunger Coalition's mission was, for OASIS and the Hospitality House, an opportunity for many potential clients to avoid the need for shelter by providing a limited source of free food, free medications, and through its faith fund, limited financial assistance for utilities when times grew temporarily tough. Many avoided the decision between which essential expenses to ignore during slumps within their household economies by accessing Coalition services. Hunger Coalition similarly offered a buffer to formerly homeless clients transitioning back into self-sufficiency while they were still living on limited resources.

In June of 2002, Rock Haven opened as a permanent care facility in response to a new project envisioned under HUD. A federal study had determined that the best way to promote its 20-year commitment to end homelessness was by dedicating a large portion of its declining funds specifically to the chronic subset of the homeless.[13] In light of the recent reduction of available funds and the effective reduction in funds due to program restructuring, Hospitality House readily saw the need among its clientele along with the need in fiscal tabulations. Because of simple arithmetic, the program was pursued. Although it did not prove to be efficient or cost effective, the new facility offered several benefits which will be discussed below.

---

[12] At this time many Baptist churches were beginning to focus efforts more on international philanthropic opportunities, sometimes at the expense of local ones. A new minister at the church at the time, coming to Hospitality House with complaints of shelter guests abusing parking, threatened angrily to withhold fiscal support if the shelter couldn't force its guests to confine their cars to the tiny lot behind the shelter. I recall that Thompson, also a Baptist minister, was saddened to be able to point out that the threat was currently empty, as the church, although supportive in many ways for many years, had not made a single contribution in well over a year.

[13] The original 20-year commitment to end homelessness has now been replaced by numerous 10-year commitments to end homelessness for certain segments of the population, usually at the community level.

In light of historical trends, it is not hard to see how this new idea of specialized care came about. States had long focused on providing aid to specialized subsets of marginalized populations. County homes and Deinstitutionalization can be viewed within a cycle of perception vacillating between community responsibility and individual rights with state or federal oversight being called upon to mediate and enforce. County Homes gave way to state institutions, which gave way to perceptions of individual rights, which forced a return to community-based services while retaining the notion of federal responsibility.

Out of the cycle emerged three primary groups seen as deserving: the elderly, the disabled, and the mentally ill. In essence, permanent supportive housing programs are designed to address chronic homelessness specifically among those groups of people in community-specified combinations. Although there are many drawbacks associated with reducing and restricting funds, removing chronic cases from emergency and transitional shelters should allow those facilities to operate more efficiently for those requiring shorter stays receiving the majority of beds.

Rock Haven was built with eight efficiency units that could spatially house 16 people with a shared laundry, kitchen, and living room. Each unit had a very small kitchenette. Applying clientele could make use of their priority status as homeless and disabled to use Section 8 vouchers to offset most of their rent. The opportunity to use other HUD program funds proved to be a loophole found through Hospitality House's relationship with NRHA, who was central in the coordination of construction and identifying and securing funds. Such use of Section 8 funds was prohibited in future agency applicants pursuing similar permanent assisted living programs.

Unfortunately, the original drawings for Rock Haven had been a proposed renovation of the Rock Annex, and the description for six two-person units. The original service grant demonstrated service to 12 people. Although the designs were updated, the technical description had not. To retain the full grant award, Rock Haven had to serve 12 people, which meant they had to come up with at least four applying couples or eight qualified individuals willing to become roommates in what were still single room rental units. Since Section 8 vouchers were allowed to be used, single individuals would have to commit to being roommates for at least one year or demonstrate together the ability to pay a rent that would have rendered the program unnecessary to them. The result was a nightmare for the staff.

In light of other problems to be described below, the decision was made to try to make the program work by serving ten people, thereby giving up a smaller portion of the grant and allowing more autonomy among the guests.[14] What looked like it could patch the hole in the budget and alleviate shelter congestion ultimately exacerbated the budgetary problem.

The landscape architect saw eight bedrooms and designed the septic system for 10 people, thereby allowing for part-time usage by staff and guests, as well as fluctuations in laundry usage. Additionally, the seasonal creek that formerly ran through the property carrying rainwater was rerouted around the property through what emerged as two right-angled turns, the first of which was coincident with a drop-off of several feet. The parking lot, to meet the code and potential use requirements, was designed with 22 spaces for a residency that could not afford cars and were mostly no longer physically capable of driving them. A change in code interpretation mid-construction required the refinishing of the interior to meet stricter fire regulations. The handicap accessibility also proved to need revamping.

When all the details had been settled, Rock Haven could house eight people for an overall construction cost of about $100,000 each. The project cost significantly more than expected, and did not fill the hole in the budget nearly as effectively as hoped. However, one positive remains to be experienced in the financing: After the program has been running for ten years, if it remains in good standing on its loans, a significant portion of Rock Haven's construction loans is eligible for forgiveness due to the incorporation of an energy efficient design.

The Coalition has not been without its share of changes during my involvement with the homeless in Watauga. Dwindling deposits to its faith fund alongside a growing at-risk population made it hard to accomplish its missions as it wanted to. Local restaurants and volunteers kept the food programs relatively stable. Its mobile pharmacy generally maintained the most commonly requested medications through donations of excess samples by numerous doctors' offices and pharmacies. Finding a pharmacist that was not already overworked and also willing to donate

---

[14] Because available funds are not legislatively stable, the HUD based programs administered through the local CoCs were granted on a 1-3 year basis, and renewable for a maximum of the original yearly amount, discounting any one time construction grants that may have been part of the first year package. Increasingly, those grants are being pushed to be renewed annually. If funds are used for construction, a twenty year commitment to provide the service is required before accepting funds.

time remained a struggle until a recent grant allowed one to be hired.

Aside from the common struggle for adequate and steady funding, space was always their biggest challenge. A food pantry needs far more storage space than most existing buildings can offer, and not many donors still provide funds for bricks and mortar projects. Thus, the facility expansion that was required at their former site on Meadowview Drive severely restricted cash flow. Two contrasting opportunities happened for the Hunger Coalition while I was involved in directing Hospitality House: the Watauga Crisis Assistance Network (WeCAN) program formed in 2002, and the Health Department outgrew its facility into a newly built one, freeing up a large county building for re-purposing in 2004.

WeCAN essentially grew out of the condition where insufficient funds existed in Hunger Coalition's Faith Fund to meet all presented needs, especially in wintertime when heating bills were high. Those in need had to approach and ask for assistance directly from multiple places in order to meet their obligations, especially to keep heat from being cut off in the wintertime. Those helping agencies included Hunger Coalition, Hospitality House, OASIS, DSS, and a variety of churches. The helping agencies had limited budgets and had to limit their per capita aid.

The churches also had limited budgets, but more importantly, their secretaries usually had limited training to assess a situation, and limited time to do so. Since church staffs depended upon the agencies for such professional guidance, clients were frequently referred back to agencies they had just visited to sign and fax confidentiality waivers allowing the two staffs to communicate and the church to pledge funds on the clients' behalf. None of these helpful organizations were close enough together to all be visited on a client's lunch break. At the time, the local bus cost 50 cents for each ride[15] and gas burned up quickly for drivers already low on funds.

Several of the churches began communicating when they noticed how much of their time and money was going directly to welfare assistance instead of to the faith fund. One church spent $18,000 on direct assistance over and above what they still consistently sent to the

---

[15] In 2004, the town of Boone agreed to follow the example of Appalachian State University and partially subsidize the standard routes offered by AppalCart, the local bus service. The standard bus routes, once free only to students, were now free to everyone. This change immediately saved the shelter about $2000 a year, and made life much easier for clients of all agencies trying to access a variety of services. The beginning of gas price escalations within that first year almost collapsed the new agreement.

local missions in the year before WeCAN was created. Agencies and churches were invited to come together around the table to discuss options. Lynne Mason, as First Presbyterian's representative, fell into the role of facilitator for the meetings early on. All agreed that a client was served best by one stop to visit with someone who could effectively and efficiently help them without jeopardizing their remaining income.

The few scam artists could be avoided, and those who could be better helped by other existing programs could be given the guidance needed regarding what was available to them from whom. The potential for saving significant funds was multi-fold: clients did not have to give up much more than their normal lunch hour to get help, reducing the likelihood that lost wages would translate into persistent need; clients could handle needs in only one or two trips, whether by car or bus; the church did not need to spend as much of their secretary's time assisting with situations he or she was not trained to assess; money was not given to people who did not really need it, or to those who had other unrealized options; and, clients with persistent problems could be guided towards making lifestyle adjustments by a skilled support staff. Since a recognized public agency was standing as guarantor for a payment, pledge arrangements could often be made over the phone, potentially saving several more client trips, and demonstrating to a variety of primary services providers that it was in their interests to encourage, or even directly support, a variety of human resources.

The only area of contention was among the churches. Some of them wanted the help to be coupled with evangelism by the contributing church. Ultimately, it was decided that an existing agency was best. Administrative funds would be minimized by piggybacking an existing support agency, and such agencies were prohibited from evangelistic activity by government-inclusive fund-seeking activities.

The last obstacle was the name. The group evinced a strong desire to have the acronym be an easily remembered positive slogan on its own. The program was restricted to Watauga County and to critical situations where necessary bills were at the point of imminent eviction or service cut-off. As the words "crisis assistance" and the idea of networking repeatedly came up, I was able to offer "WeCAN" – for Watauga Crisis Assistance Network – if the group was willing to accept the lowercase 'e' having no real purpose in the acronym.[16] In short work

---

[16] I had been invited to the meetings due to my role as facilitator of the InterAgency Council meetings offered by the Volunteer Outreach Center (VOC). Those meetings allowed a variety of topics to be discussed by all attending community service agencies, and for those same

it was settled, mostly through the faith community's desire to help the whole community while continuing to effectively support the agencies around the table.

Agencies attending the meetings were asked to submit a brief request if they wanted to be considered as host, or if they wanted to recommend another as host, outlining why. The Hunger Coalition submitted a brief request primarily because they had filled the role through the Faith Fund for a number of years, and Hospitality House submitted a request because several churches had voiced the opinion that it was in the more visibly accessible location and closer to other assisting agencies along the same bus route. No other agencies were expected to make a proposal, and none did.

Hospitality House was awarded the contract at the final task meeting in October of 2002. The first two individuals, referred by Hunger Coalition, were helped the same day although the program did not officially start until November. The Community Faith Fund was laid to rest. In December, Lynne Mason, who had clearly demonstrated her dedication to the cause as the unofficial chair of the task meetings, was asked to apply her MSW (Masters of Social Work) degree as the part time director for the new crisis assistance program.

In 2003, the ever-refining transitional shelter grant Thompson had garnered for the Sleeping Place became strict enough that Hospitality House could no longer house two disparate programs in the same building, despite a complete separation of facilities. By definition, many of the guests of the winter shelter could have also qualified as transitional guests, but many others could not have been. Confusion over the budgetary ramifications and documentation requirements of a divergent perception of programs was a big part of the problem.

From HUD and OEO perspective, there were only two programs recognized by the grants: emergency and transitional. In much simplified terms, if a client stayed over thirty days and was properly documented in a location previously accepted for the purpose, transitional funds could be spent on their services. Locally, there were three programs recognized in two different facilities: emergency, transitional, and seasonal or crisis. The seasonal program was weather dependant, focused on those unwilling to qualify for access to the other programs, and, therefore, not well documented. Even in the same space, seasonal guests could

---

agencies to remain aware of what each was doing. Since VOC was officially a program of HCUW and I worked for HH as Operations Director, I could be called upon by each to clarify details, or speak to the concerns of each agency if their representatives were running late or unable to attend.

potentially be charged to either program grant, but many guests would have chosen to freeze before they would sit long enough to answer all the questions required. Many others were too inebriated to complete documentation, even if they were willing. Although clients could be served without being counted for grant purposes, the extra level of tracking would have become tedious for such a small staff and could have threatened grant funds if non-documentation became a popular request for guests preferring to minimize buy-in to what many marginalized individuals nebulously consider as "the system" or "the man" when answering too many personal questions.

At the same time, stricter enforcement of fire and building codes was determining that the long-standing special-use permission was no longer to be considered and the numbers of people that were being housed were being forced to decline. The 22 people we had been sheltering in the emergency shelter was reduced initially to 15, although a closer look at how the space was divided allowed it to rise again to 17 as long as the overnight volunteer remained awake. The Sleeping Place, which occasionally reached to over thirty people in the wintertime, was found to be adequate for only about 13.

When, as mentioned above, the Sleeping Place converted completely to transitional housing, we gave up the winter shelter program and reduced aid to many seasonal and transient clienteles. It was taken as a kindness that the code inspections were conducted early in the year, when the maximum amount of time was available to pursue alternatives for the following year's winter program. Although no alternatives emerged as viable, an arrangement was reached with public safety agencies whereby we could slightly exceed capacity in the emergency shelter building on severe nights by calling the sheriffs' department – where the 911 dispatch was housed – and alerting them of the greater potential for injury in the event of a fire. On such nights, the overnight manager had to take extra care to stay awake.

Service coordinators worked extra hard at trying to find nearby overflow shelter that could last from around Halloween until around Easter as one plan after another fell through. A couple of the nearby churches did experiment with methods of sheltering small numbers of people on demand, but the sporadic nature of such need proved unwieldy for both staffs. The knowledge that the shelter would not be available that year helped a few of the repeat guests find alternative arrangements, some for the better, and some for much worse, while the presence of a temporary Greyhound bus depot allowed many of the transient guests to keep on their way without getting stranded for a night or two. Sherwood Forest still enjoyed a lively population that winter.

Most of the former Coalition of Churches had relocated their facilities away from downtown as the University and business district grew hungry for space. They were thus not conveniently located to assist as they once could, although Grace Lutheran, who had an agreement with the Red Cross to provide on demand crisis shelter in an emergency, routinely explored creative ways to assist where it was able. There was also, at least for a couple of years, a renewed increase in the correlation between extremely cold weather and the ability of late working staff members in various churches to remember to lock certain doors. Discretionary funding was once again increasingly being spent on the cheaper rooms of more compassionate hotels and the Mann Travelers' Fund was being expended within days of each new allocation.

A 100-year flood in Rock Haven's first year immediately clogged a roadside drainage culvert uphill. The storm run-off undermined one of the three handicapped ramps, part of the septic system and a large chunk of the parking lot. The water rushing downhill did not slow down to make the first right-turn and ignored the drop-off completely, trying to follow its original path. The building itself proved to be extremely sound, however, as only a gallon or two of water was forced under double basement doors only a few feet away from the severely compromised septic system. With no one apparently at fault for that unexpected damage, Hospitality House spent another $26,000 in repairs. With the culvert so recently maintained, the second 100-year flood the following year only damaged the creek bed and partially undermined an electric pole by the road.

The upside is that eight people who would normally have been trying to meet long-term needs in a short-term shelter program were living in permanent assistive housing and therefore not occupying higher demand shelter beds when winter came on. One of them was paid as a resident manager for performing routine maintenance functions and providing light supervision when service coordinators were not on site. Additionally, the temporary passage of the Greyhound bus service through town allowed many transients to keep on their way instead of pausing briefly for winter shelter, thereby reducing the need further.

When the Health Department outgrew its location proximate to Bamboo Road and moved into a new facility built for the purpose above the Department of Social Services, it was determined as preferable that the vacated building should benefit the non-profit sector, preferably housing multiple agencies.[17] Hospitality House and Hunger Coalition expressed the strongest interest in occupying the building, in part because Caldwell Community College (CCC&TI) offered classes next-door, and the location was convenient to nearby Bradford Park, a location commonly in need of outreach from one or both of the agencies. Residents of the area suffered from efficient transportation to adequately access services. It was soon discovered that the building required too much work to outfit for residential use, but with a bit of spatial creativity, it could easily be made to work for Hunger Coalition. The County was hopeful that there would be room for several smaller agencies, another feature that could not have worked well in a shelter scenario. Thus, Hunger Coalition would move again in 2005, this time hopefully for good. Breaking with traditions, the move this time would not be forced, and one of the many realty offices of the area now occupies their vacated space.

When in 2005, it was decided that Jim Thompson would retire and Lynne Mason would become the acting Executive Director, I had determined I was going to give up my position as Director of Operations in order to return to school to pursue this research. Two new federal grants were in the works that would completely change the way the shelter handled programs. In the wake of events surrounding Rock Haven, financial stability was becoming more important than client welfare among a small sector of the board of directors. Individual politics were coming into play. Rather than trying to learn several new programs under a new boss and a changing board with very different and internally conflicting perspectives, I retired from paid work with the homeless in order to do research on the subject instead. Most of the staff at the time and several of the board members also quickly found less stressful opportunities for their skills.

Around this time, Marian Peters (personal communication, March 28, 2006), a physics professor at ASU, had decided to create a new clinic to help those who had neither insurance nor a regular doctor. Peters took a sabbatical from teaching and trained as a Physician's Assistant. Soon after I began classes, she began screening individuals with unaddressed health concerns in the evenings. Hospitality House made space available in their offices, and Peters began networking

---

[17] A former business incubator had closed down a few years earlier. It had sheltered several smaller non-profits, most of whom had relocated as part of a prolonged close down process. The community had expressed a strong desire for a non-profit incubator, and was actively exploring options.

among local doctors and other medically related practitioners to develop a plan of action, both for individuals served and a permanent location for her proposed clinic.

Providing a fortuitous connection, the unused space at the Hunger Coalition building had been arranged by the former Health Department for medical purposes. The Hunger Coalition board decided not only to provide the space to the new Community Care Clinic, but also to absorb it under its umbrella by reforming itself as the Hunger and Health Coalition. As OASIS had done over two decades earlier, the Community Care Clinic soon pursued its own charitable, not-for-profit (IRS Statute 501c3) status (Peters, 2006; C. Winebarger, personal communication, April, 2008).

In August 2007, Serenity Farms closed the doors of its residential substance abuse program due to infrastructural issues with the building. Although several of its former clients are continuing their program in a variety of scattered home sites, many more of them are left without adequate guidance, and no new clients can be admitted (R. Cox, personal communication, October 29, 2007). Leading the community search for a new site are Robert Cox, who has been active with the various high-risk populations in Watauga for over a decade, and the newly hired Housing Coordinator for NRBH, Lori Watts. Watts (personal communication, summer, 2008) recently informed me that a smaller version of Serenity Farms is being developed for reintroduction soon.

The Northwestern Regional Housing Authority (NRHA) has not been dormant throughout this time. Its influence on the homeless population is somewhat more nebulous. Its Section 8 and White Laurel Programs prevent many people, especially families, from becoming homeless. HUD guidelines inherently give preferences to those who are disabled or homeless and have no safe alternatives to the shelter or living without habitation. They are currently actively working with about 400 households in Watauga County out of an office with only one field officer. Not quite 40% of those are on the waiting list, and just above 10% are at White Laurel.

Additionally, the NRHA is instrumental in the creation of the programs proposed through the Continuum of Care, which has traditionally met within their administrative offices. Those projects relatively recently include Rock Haven, Wintergreen, a similar program in Wilkes, as well as several others in neighboring counties. It is currently aiding in the development and seeking of funds for the proposed new shelter for Hospitality House.

Now, the housing crisis in the county is worse than ever before. Email conversations (October 29, 2007) with Ned Fowler at NRHA and Jennifer Herman at OASIS bring to light that the combination of rapid development, escalating property demands, water shortages, and the expansion of the University's student population has placed such a burden on the market that landlords are routinely asking more than "fair market" value for their rents. A 99% occupancy rate meant that, despite a temporarily short wait time for Section 8 voucher availability (2-3 months as opposed to 12-24), 40 voucher recipients at the end of October, 2007 were still unable to find housing that charged at or below fair market rates.

This appalling condition is made worse by the fact that there is presently not enough source-water available to allow the development of new affordable housing. Even if there were, developers in the area are only interested in producing housing to attracting seasonal second-home residents and preying on the student population's need for housing at any cost close to the campus. The brief availability of quickly issued Section 8 vouchers allowed by slow-to-be-approved federal changes in HUD funding in 2007 has dried up in 2008, returning the wait time for Section 8 recipients to over a year, a situation that is still much better than in larger urban areas (T. Barse & J. Parker, personal communication, May 15, 2008; Fowler, 2008).

Fair Market rent on a two bedroom apartment is now $718/ month (Fair Market Rents, 2007), up from $575 only five years ago. The housing wage needed to afford such an apartment in 2006 was $12.79/hr (Nicholson, 2006b) or $23,000 a year. Fifty-eight percent of county residents fell below that level in 2006 (Nicholson, 2006b). To afford current Fair Market rents, all such households need to earn $28,720 annually, or $13.80 per hour, year round. This is roughly twice the minimum wage. Most local property owners now charge more than Fair Market, making them ineligible to work with Section 8, even if they were otherwise inclined to.

Those seeking to buy a house in the area can expect an even greater assault on their finances. The median price paid for a home in the 3rd quarter of 2007 was already over $300,000 and preliminary data for the final quarter suggested a jump of another $50,000 was likely. That figure was up from a median of only $200,000 in 2004 (City-Data.com, 2005). This research has already pointed out that it is now virtually impossible to buy a house for less than $150,000 anywhere in the county.

On the surface, owning a home in Watauga County looks easy. Of 26,564 households in 2006, 62.9% of them owned their homes. The 2000 census tells us that the average household size in the county is 2.26 (U. S. Census Bureau, 2000a). Presuming that has not changed significantly, the math gives us an adjusted household population of 60,035 individuals (141% of the permanent population), or roughly 17,335 people not part of the actual county population. Thus, only 71% of the households in the county are occupied year round. When the 29% seasonal occupancy rate is subtracted from the total households, it can be seen that roughly 2/3 of the local population are tenants. Roughly 1/3 of tenants are students. Although the students are counted among year round residents, the commitment level of most of them is minimal and transitory.

Becoming a homeowner is not an easy objective for those escaping homeless in the area. With 141% of the total population competing for space in a saturated housing market, landlords are easily commanding more than fair market value, meaning that even if assistance is sought and qualified for through Section 8, it will be hard to find a landlord that will settle for the level of rent guaranteed by joining the program. What development that is being approved during the current water shortage is taking advantage of the increased interests of seasonal homeowners, who are not dependent upon local wages, in order to maximize profits.

Recent Statistical Record

Aside from one unpublished report by Ian Mance (2005) on the homeless of Watauga County and a handful of internal documents, also unpublished, from the various agencies, there does not appear to be any literature of a local nature relating to homelessness. The Mance essay compiles statistics from the documented shelter guests of Hospitality House of Boone from 1994 – 2004.

Mance placed Watauga County in rural America, where the percentage of those living below the poverty line is 15.9%, an average higher than both national and urban figures (Mance, 2005). At the beginning of this chapter, I shared that roughly 18% of Watauga's residents subsist on sub-poverty incomes, and that although Boone is an urban center for the surrounding area, the county itself is still rural by nature. Watauga County also matches Mance's findings that rural homeless are often hidden in forgotten barns and similar places, are most often White, and are more often first time victims of homelessness (Mance, 2005). Thus, Watauga matches most rural trends. Unlike the national trend, however, Mance found that single women did not make up the largest group among the homeless, even when taking the presence of OASIS into consideration (Mance, 2005). Single men appeared to be the overwhelming majority of homeless.

Mance's study identified Hospitality House as the primary shelter for the homeless of a seven county area, located in a county then offering a 1.9% unemployment rate, coupled with low wages and high rents (meaning high underemployment is the norm). All of this is attributable in some degree to the local university or to what amounts to absentee landholders – second or seasonal homeowners. A strong dependency on seasonal employment was likewise noted among shelter guests. This was partially attributable to the increased marketability of college-educated students, combined with the willingness of many of those students to work for lower wages, and without benefits, while in school (Mance, 2005). It was cheaper for employers to hire students.

At the time of the study, the shelter had served about 8000 individuals during its 20 years of operation and boasted only 17 beds in 2005, turning away an overflow nightly when weather was temperate. An additional capacity of 12- 15 was served through a transitional (long-term) housing program, with 8-10 more housed in a permanent shelter program (Mance, 2005).

A basic breakdown of his survey yielded a 72:28 male: female ratio with an average age of 35. Males were marginally older than females. Only 2% of records constituted guests over 60 years of age. Children were not considered guests of the facility and thus were not factored into statistics.[18] Nearly two-thirds (63%) of guests had a high school diploma or GED and 26% had attended at least some college. Males were more likely to have acquired high school equivalencies, but women who went to college were more likely to complete the secondary degree. Nearly three-fourths (72%) were unemployed at the time of entrance into emergency shelter. Addiction was lower at the shelter than the nationally cited average among homeless, although men were still more likely to be addicts than women, and veterans significantly more so than non-veterans (Mance, 2005).

---

[18] The current trend is for non-emancipated children accompanied by at least one legal guardian to remain as wards of those guardians so long as the guardian/s continue appropriate care for their child/ren while they themselves receive aid, including such aid as is available on the children's behalf. Un-emancipated minors without guardians must enter foster care.

The very first thing one notices when looking at the population data reported by Hospitality House (Table 3.2) is that the need for beds is rising. The average daily occupancy (ADO) rose by three beds in just two years. Such a rise equals over 1000 added annual bed-nights. Looking at the total number served, we can tell that the number of individuals being served is also going up, but slowly. One of the reasons for this is that, despite transitional and permanent shelter providing an additional ADO of 19 beds in 2005, the length of stay required at the Emergency Shelter is still increasing. Since ADO must be a whole number, the math does not allow the exact factoring of length of stay, but it appears to have risen from roughly 24 days in 2005 to over 27 in 2007.

Table 3.2: *Gender and Shelter Population in Watauga County*

	ADO	Singles			# of fams	Adults in fams			Kids in fams			Total served		
		M	F	T		M	F	T	M	F	T	M	F	T
HH-ESG 04-05	14	132	35	167	20	9	20	29	13	4	17	154	59	213
HH-ESG 05-06	16	147	39	186	15	9	14	23	10	6	16	166	59	225
HH-ESG 06-07	17	158	39	197	12	12	11	23	7	1	8	177	51	228
HH-94-05												1080	420	1500
OASIS												0	53	53
HH SURVEY	33													242

Sources are: The 2004-2005 ESG Annual Report filed by Hospitality House; The 2005-2006 ESG Annual Report filed by Hospitality House; The 2006-2007 Annual Report filed by Hospitality House (Mason, personal communication, 2008); Hospitality House data compiled by Ian Mance (2005) cumulative for years 1994-2005; Interview with OASIS director Jennifer Herman (2006); 2005 Appalachian Homeless Service Provider Survey returned by Hospitality House.

Notes on abbreviations: ADO = Average Daily Occupancy; M= Males; F= Females; T= Total M and F; fams = families

The primary data I was interested in from this table was the male to female ratio. Mance had observed a ratio of 72 males for every 28 females staying at the shelter (Mance, 2005), and I was curious if that was changing. I found that the year immediately after Mance's study (2004-2005) still matched up perfectly with his findings regardless of whether children were included or excluded. Singles alone proved a ratio of 79 males to 21 females, a variance explained by the predominance of male children sheltered in that year. Both trends hold true in all three fiscal years completed since Mance's study. The percentage of children in the shelter declined sharply, however, so the overall male female ratio climbed from 71.9% in 2005 to 77.3% by 2007.

The predominance of male adults extended in 2007 to single parent house-holds as well, as more males were documented in familial situations than females. As Mance suggested, part of the reason for such female under-representation was the existence of OASIS. Although a survey was not collected from OASIS, an interview with the Jennifer Herman (2006) indicated that they had provided shelter to 53 women during the year ending in 2005. When those 53 women are included in the 2005 tabulations, the male: female ratio drops to 57.6% male overall as compared to 56.6% of adults.

It should be noted that OASIS does not exclude males from accessing the majority of their services. Only about 20% of those served by OASIS require sheltered assistance, which is offered in a variety of locations under the same emergency and transitional shelter guidelines employed by Hospitality House. Herman shares that although males seldom request such aid in Watauga County, they can sometimes be accommodated in OASIS's shelters and can always be assisted in hotels when a combination of genders would not otherwise be avoidable (Herman, 2006). Similar concerns could arise if males present to support groups. Males in domestic violence situations may prefer to find shelter at Hospitality House. If this is true, they also have not been claiming domestic violence as a cause in the last three report years.

The data so far begs the question: If single women, with or without children, are the largest segment of homeless in America; and, rural areas are generating larger than their share of homeless; and, Boone is the urban center of an otherwise rural area; why is the percentage of women so low in the local record? That the shelter long desired a separate home for women suggests that the need was observable within the community at one time. That men do not approach OASIS for aid even if they have been abused suggests that the converse may also be true: single women do not approach Hospitality House if they can ignore or otherwise respond to their homelessness. Men do approach Hospitality House, as is abundantly clear from all statistics. Additionally, OASIS (53) and Hospitality House (55) sheltered adult women almost equally in 2005.

Cities do tend to catch people seeking opportunities and aid not available in their own communities. The lack of overall shelter space and a women's shelter in Watauga may be causing some women to be relocating when they need shelter, especially when they have children in their care. An inability to arrange stable childcare was an obstacle during my employment at the shelter. Many parents continued to access severely strained family resources for that purpose, or struggled to maintain or even acquire jobs because their time was already too much in demand. Our society overwhelmingly favors retaining maternal childcare relations when marital partnerships fail, a factor that ensures that most single parents will be female. Additionally, although it appears to have improved significantly in recent years, women are still likely to be compensated less in today's employment market. Thus, better access to childcare, and/or a women's shelter might prove Watauga closer to the national statistics.

Of a more measurable nature, Northwestern Regional Housing Authority offers additional insight. Households headed by single women are by far the most common recipient of Section 8 aid at 78%. Neither NRHA nor HUD guidelines offer preferences based on gender or marital status, which means that single mothers are the norm because they are the most common presenters to NRHA programs. Retention of even strained family social resources increases the likelihood that those in need will not have to access shelter in order to get help. If a desire for increased child welfare provides social capital, then single mothers may also be able to leverage otherwise strained family relations long enough to avoid shelters while they seek housing opportunities. Although HUD does offer a homelessness preference, those who can access social resources for shelter do not qualify, so an accurate homelessness comparison cannot be made.

In Table 3.3, data are compared regarding a variety of problems presented by clients that resulted in homelessness. Over time, the list of options suggested by grantors has expanded and contracted, and in most cases prefers that only the primary presented problem be tabulated in their reports. Shelters need to know all reasons if they are to effectively help guests return to stable housing. As a result, the means of documenting those problems has fluctuated over time. Consequently, the data compiled by Mance is especially difficult to compare to the more recent report data. Concepts such as "dual diagnosis" - which designates both mental and substance issues- and "underemployment," were not recognized until recently.

Lifestyle changes such as eviction, transience, relocation, and release from prison were similarly discounted as means of becoming homeless. It was often once seen as easier to consider most of these and permanent disability simply as forms of unemployment, despite the need to address each situation differently. It is clear from the table that,

Table 3.3: *Presented Triggers for Homelessness in Watauga County*

		Reason for Homelessness										
	MI	Al c	Dr	D D	DV -M	DV -F	UN	UN D	E V	P r	T r	Re l	Di s
HH-ESG 04-05	14	28	7	41		10	22	7	18	15	14	27	5
HH-ESG 05-06	21	21	11	46		14	15	14	22	21	6	17	16
HH-ESG 06-07	32	18	37	89		6	15	2	1	19	6		3
HH-94-05					15	94							
OASIS 05					0	53							
HH Survey -05	224	500	302				1086						

Sources are: The 2004-2005 ESG Annual Report filed by Hospitality House; The 2005-2006 ESG Annual Report filed by Hospitality House; The 2006-2007 Annual Report filed by Hospitality House (L. Mason, personal communication, 21 October, 2008); Hospitality House data compiled by Ian Mance (Mance) cumulative for years 1994-2005; Interview with OASIS director Jennifer Herman (2006); 2005 Appalachian Homeless Service Provider Survey returned by Hospitality House.

Notes on abbreviations: MI = mental illness; Alc = alcohol abuse; Dr = non-alcohol drug abuse; DD = dual diagnosis; DV = domestic violence- male (M) or female (F); UN = unemployment; UND = underemployment; EV = eviction; Pr = release from prison; Tr = transient; Rel = relocation; and Dis = disabled homeless population.

during the course of the ten-year sample, unemployment, at 72.4%, was the option of choice for service coordinators of the era.

After unemployment, Mance found that alcohol abuse (33.3%), drug abuse (20.1%), mental illness (14.9%), and domestic violence (7.3%) were the four most commonly tracked problems resultant in homelessness in Watauga (Mance, 2005). There were 48% more problems reported than there were people presenting, outlining the fact that homelessness is often due to a confluence of situations arising to affect one's stability.

Taken together, the three report years following Mance's study have seen the introduction of dual diagnosis, which became by far the primary presenter at 26.4%. Alcoholism (11.6%), mental illness (10.1%), and drug abuse (8.3%) still lead the pack. Mental illness rises to an actual rate of 36.5% when you factor in dual diagnosis. Alcohol and drug abuse would both have higher actual percentages as well, but there is no way to distinguish whether drugs, alcohol, or both contributed to a diagnosis of dual diagnosis. Surprisingly, release from prison (8.3%) is right up there with them. Unemployment drops to only 7.8%. The accuracy of all of these ratios is called into question by the fact that the reports they were gleaned from only provided the primary cause of homelessness. Secondary or tertiary reasons are not noted, thus all actual rates may be higher. Most of them will be.

During the 2006 Point in Time Count, an annual attempt by North Carolina's Continuums of Care to quantify homelessness within their districts, I contacted the local prisons to see if they could answer what percentage of their populations would add to the homeless population. Two of the four prisons contacted were quite helpful. Their details offered a formula used to provide such data. They both found that it generally proves accurate in the long term. The formula yielded 2% of the total population, or a maximum of less than forty people from all four prisons in Region D who would have no place to go upon release.

Although the numbers presented by Hospitality House between 2004 and 2007 suggest a higher rate of prisoners than the prisons themselves would seem to indicate, the discrepancy can be partly explained by the tendency to include both release from local jails as well as prisons in the tabulation. Prisons also do not discharge all of their prisoners locally, meaning that some prisoners to the region may have been incarcerated in the larger prisons elsewhere in the state. In cold months especially, some homeless unable to find socially accepted sheltered space commit relatively minor infractions solely to facilitate a night or two in jail.

I was surprised to see that domestic violence had fallen to only the eighth most common obstacle presented at the shelter in 2005. Factoring in the women for OASIS increased the overall percentage to 23.7% in the county. When the combined data are viewed for women alone, it was still clearly the primary cause of homelessness that year at 51.6%. In both examinations including OASIS, domestic violence placed above everything but mental illness as determined through the combination of mental illness alone plus dual diagnosis. Overall mental illness, as a primary presenter, rose from 25.8% in 2005 to 53.8% in 2007. In general, the three-year trend shows a consistent rise in mental illness, drug use, dual diagnosis, and, among the female population, domestic violence. Alcohol alone is on the decline, along with unemployment, transience, and relocation, which disappeared completely in 2007. Without being able to observe the data compiled by Mance as it changed from year to year, there is no way yet to identify if these are long-term trends. It is possible that the trends are part of the urbanization process being experienced by Boone itself, or simply a result of changing screening methods under new management and new grant requirements. Certainly, unemployment has defaulted its dominant status.

Table 3.4: *Veteran Status, Race, and Ethnicity in Watauga County*

| | Veteran | | Race/Ethnicity | | | | | | total served |
	M	F	As	Bl	Wh	Hi	N.Am	BiR	
HH-ESG 04-05	32	2	0	12	184	5	6	6	213
HH-ESG 05-06	21	0	1	19	186	3	10	5	224
HH-ESG 06-07	25	1	0	6	198	6	5	3	228
Survey 05	35	2	0	15	208	5	7	7	242
HH 1995-2004	260	25							1500
OASIS									53

Sources are: The 2004-2005 ESG Annual Report filed by Hospitality House; The 2005-2006 ESG Annual Report filed by Hospitality House; The 2006-2007 Annual Report filed by Hospitality House (Mason, personal communication, 2008); Hospitality House data compiled by Ian Mance (2005) cumulative for years 1994-2005; Interview with OASIS director Jennifer Herman (2006); 2005 Appalachian Homeless Service Provider Survey returned by Hospitality House.

Notes on abbreviations used: M=Male; F=Female; As = Asian; Bl = Black; Wh = White; Hi = Hispanic; N.Am = Native American; BiR= Biracial

The declines in particular may be the result of the increased demands of the local population. As the housing market becomes more expensive, preventing even professional level job seekers from being able to find homes in their price range, relocation and transient exploration of the area would reasonably become less attractive.

Mance found a surprisingly high representation of veterans in the shelter. The survey sent out throughout Appalachia also demonstrated that the area is more attractive to veterans than I had realized while employed at the shelter. Table 3.4 outlines what was discovered in regards to veteran status, as well as the racial demographics of the last three years. In regards to the 2005 survey, it is obvious that it disagrees with the ESG report of the same year. This discrepancy is explained by the fact that the ESG report only speaks to the emergency shelter level of care, while the survey details were inclusive of guests in transitional and permanent shelter programs. The reporting cycle for that program ends at a different time during the year. The shelter representative responding to the survey acknowledged the complexity of combining the statistics, but did not identify the method of resolution employed. See Appendix C for an example of the survey, which will be discussed in detail in the next chapter.

Mance found that 19% of his sample was comprised of veterans, which equated to 24% of the male guests and 6% of the female guests (Mance, 2005). The survey found that 15.3% of all fiscal year 2005 Hospitality House guests were veterans, although the attempt to provide cumulative gender and population demographics proved unusable. The survey data does closely correlate with the ESG report for the same year, for which 17.1% of adults proved veterans comprising 3.6% of the adult female population and 22.7% of the adult male population. Since adding in the longer-term guests increases the overall rate, veterans are more common in Hospitality House's longer-term care programs, suggesting veterans in Watauga County face greater obstacles than many to maintaining stable housing. There is no bias in favor of veterans in service provision.

When it comes to race and ethnicity, it is not surprising that the two data sets for 2005 show very little variation. With a difference of only 29 individuals reported, the largest variation is only .6% on Blacks, comprising 5.6% of emergency shelter guests and 6.2% of guests in the longer-term facilities. Whites comprised 86% of emergency shelter guests and 86.4% of all guests. Native Americans and those of mixed race each comprised 2.8% of emergency shelter guests and 2.9% of all guests, while Hispanics represented the smallest segment at 2.3% of emergency shelter guests as compared to 2.1% of all guests.

It is possible to extrapolate guests sheltered outside of the emergency shelter. Whites comprise 82.8% of the total, followed by Blacks at 10.3%, and Native Americans and Biracial individuals show at 3.4% each. Hispanics disappear. The numbers are not conclusive however, as one person equals 3.4%, and only 5:29 people were other than White.

The small numbers of minorities in the shelter is a bit misleading for those who are used to looking at demographics for larger cities. In the 2000 Census, Watauga County was comprised of 96.5% Whites, 1.6% Blacks, 0.6% Asians, 0.6% Biracial, and only 0.3% Native American. 1.5% of the total racial breakdown was also of Hispanic ethnicity (Regional Business Services Team, 2005). Census Bureau estimates for 2006 were not much changed, demonstrating a population of 42,700 individuals comprised of 94.1% non-Hispanic Whites, 2% Blacks, 0.3% Native American, 0.8% Asian, 0.8% Bi-racial, and 1.9% Hispanic. All minorities except Native Americans were on the rise.

When 2006 county statistics were compared to 2005 Hospitality House demographics, it emerges that Asians are unlikely to become homeless in the county. Despite their prevalence in numbers, Whites are the next lowest with only 0.46% of the county's population in shelter, followed by 0.62% of Hispanics. Native Americans are the most likely to need shelter with 5.47% of their numbers seeking shelter, while Blacks (1.75%) and those of mixed races (2.05%) fall in the middle of the observable range. Percentages of minorities in the shelter are higher than those for the county as a whole demonstrating that minorities in Watauga find themselves at an unequal disadvantage, a common situation in both urban and rural environments.

Local Causes of Homelessness

A common set of conversations among local homeless service providers relates to the dichotomy of effects wrought by both the growing university campus, and the growing recreational home populations in the town and county. On the one hand, both populations provide potential volunteers and donors, as well as a demand for increased job opportunities alongside increasing cultural understanding, opportunities, and diversity. At the same time, they – the students especially – help foster community awareness of a variety of issues.

On the other hand, such growth in transient residency promotes competition for nearby commercial properties, which raises values to a level that makes competition and long-term success nearly impossible for small business owners and non-professionals. The majority of the new jobs are unskilled low-wage and/or seasonal ones. Moreover, some of the issues brought to light translate into legislative decisions that go against the desires of permanent residents.

Residential properties undergo similar hyper-valuation as landlords compensate their rents to accommodate the summer student exodus while property developers target a market willing to pay more than long-time residents, especially non-professionals, can afford. Individuals facing challenges to personal transportation find it nearly impossible to find affordable housing close to services.

Since about 1998, the Town has essentially retained an even third of the county's official population (Currie, 1998). However, Appalachian State University has entered into active recruitment towards increasing its population along with its share of North Carolina University system funding, and developers are actively recruiting wealthy seasonal residency through a leap in the production of high-end housing units. The effect is the replacement of generational homeowners with seasonal ones, and a percentage decline in county residency coupled with a rise in student residency.

One developer began offering houses in 2006 for over one million dollars in a new development in the eastern part of the county, while realtors cite the unavailability of houses for under $150,000 countywide (Nicholson, 2006a). That same developer currently lists vacant lots as low as $450,000 (Ginn Resorts at Laurelmor, 2008). Listings have recently been posted for as much as $750,000 per lot. Underscoring this trend are the facts that the housing market is saturated at 99% and effective residency is roughly 141%, which will be discussed below.

For those providing services to prevent or ameliorate homelessness, the reality is that such a transient overall population neither has nor offers strong social networking connections. Sprawling communities that once took care of each other by providing sustenance and opportunities have largely been replaced by suburban neighborhoods and seasonal enclaves where most neighbors barely know each other and the majority of businesses no longer see employees as long-term resources integrated with family units.

For those with long-term ties to the area, hereditary skills of local self-sufficiency have largely been outmoded by market potentials with no individual preparation for the transition. Many such individuals make a parallel transition from landowner to tenant in the hopes that relocation will inherently involve adequate access to new opportunities. Regardless of whether or not that relocation or transition occurs, the children of the self-displaced generation grow up without the benefit of established family and community patterns to guide in complete assimilation. Both generations remain at high risk of poverty and an increased risk of homelessness and intergenerational conflict. Most of those newly made tenants do not remain in the communities where they have the deepest social ties. At the least, they move from county to town, but often they even change counties. Wataugans leave to find a better rent to income ratio, while outsiders move into the county seeking perceived opportunities they did not have at home.

Add to that the fact that towns and cities offer the perception of unlimited opportunity to those residing in more rural surrounding areas. Attempts to make Boone and the surrounding towns more attractive to temporary residents also attract those that do not fit the desired profile. The call to new residents reaches those desiring to start their own businesses, those who live in areas of higher unemployment, and those who want a change and do not realize that they may not be able to access the same resources wherever they may decide to go at the same level they are used to.

Unemployment in Watauga County in 2005 was rated at 3.3%. This compares to a 5.3% rate in North Carolina and 5.2% nationally. Census data in 2000 showed an employment rate of only 57.4% in Watauga County with an additional 16.3% of the population under 18 years of age (Regional Business Services Team, 2005). The employment rate includes working minors and any retirees who may still be employed.

What is not pointed out in those statistics is a remainder of at least an additional 23% of the population not working due to disability, lack of motivation, retirement or inability to find a job while looking through the Employment Security Commission (ESC) databases. Many of these individuals, plus many of the minors, may in fact recognize themselves as unemployed but depend solely on opportunities posted in newspapers, help wanted signs, or the variety of online jobs boards such as craigslist.com, or monster.com, none of which contribute data to unemployment statistics.

Also not presented in the statistics is underemployment. Just like unemployment, which is adjusted routinely to account for seasonal and temporary employment, there is no easy way to calculate underemployment. Around 2000, my fellow staff at Hospitality House and I estimated that the underemployment rate, a contributing problem for many of our clients at the time, was roughly 40% countywide. An article appearing in a local newspaper in 2006 stated that 58% of individuals living in Watauga County could not afford to do so (Nicholson, 2006b), which suggests that the underemployment rate may be even higher now. Thus, for a variety of reasons, presenting a seemingly low unemployment rate may be luring individuals into unfamiliar communities where they are going to have a hard time succeeding, even if they do find a job.

Outlook for the Future

When all is said and done, the outlook for homeless service provision in Watauga is bleak but stable. The programs available are generally comprised of dedicated staffs who honestly want to help their clients make a better life for themselves. Although a growing town focused on economic advancement is driving up the incidence of homelessness, bed-space is successfully being created in hopes of keeping ahead of demand while facilitating more efficient methods of meeting varied needs.

Unfortunately, and despite NRHA efforts to the contrary, the community is not keeping up with the need for affordable housing. In fact, virtually all development in the area seems intent on exacerbating that need by focusing efforts on attracting a wealthier but more transient population. Although residential and other tourists, along with the jobs they create, only stay for a short time each year, the increases in property value and infrastructural costs are shared with the permanent residency year-round.

Excessive inefficient development in the recent past has contributed significantly to a situation where water shortages and inappropriate development competes for limited and even unavailable resources, leaving nearly 60% of the populace struggling to make ends meet, and nearly twenty percent with no hope of doing so on their own.

With all the moving around agencies have been doing recently, services relevant to homelessness victims are coalescing into several loci around town. The development of such centers is both fortuitous and telling. They are fortuitous in that proximity facilitates support networks for providers, including the potential for increased corroboration, resource sharing, and a reduction of burn-out. For clients accessing similar services, less time is spent running around town, and facilitation of any necessary cross communication is made easier.

There are essentially four focal points for the homeless to be aware of. The first is the Human Services Complex on Poplar Grove Connector, quite close to the Court House, probation and parole, and the public library. The complex itself contains New River Behavioral Healthcare, the Department of Social Services, Project on Aging, and the Health Department, all accessible from a single parking area. For the most part, the County supports these programs without reservation, and actively participated in the creation of the center. It is also common for clients accessing the majority of them to view their treatments as punitive.

The next center contains primarily standard preventive measures, and is not quite so close together. Northwestern Regional Housing Authority, the Employment Security Commission, JobLink, Vocational Rehabilitation, and the headquarters for AppalCart, the local bus service, are all located near the junction of highways 321, 105, and the 105-Extension. Although crossing any of the highways requires a level of courage and luck, travel between several of these agencies on a lunch hour would not be that difficult. The Boone Mall - where a bus can be picked up traveling as far as Winston-Salem - and New River Light and Power are also handy to this location. Services in this area are well tolerated by local governments, but generally ignored, drawing most of their charter and funds from larger governmental input. The partial exception is AppalCart, which depends primarily on the town of Boone and Appalachian State University for funding.

The third center is primarily medical in nature. It contains the hospital and quite a number of general and specialized doctors' offices, including an Urgent Care clinic frequently used by employers and human services for drug screening, and Deerfield Pharmacy, which carries a lot of specialized medical equipment. Of potentially greater interest to many in danger of homelessness is the new Family Resource Center, immediately behind Deerfield Pharmacy, which houses WAMY, OASIS, and the Children's Council. Some remaining unused space does not preclude the potential for other agencies moving in. Such proximity to medical aid could be quite helpful to domestic violence victims seeking emergency assistance from OASIS, and those seeking medical aid for DV incidents are more likely to take steps towards breaking the cycle with guidance so close to treatment.

Lastly, the final locus developing is of relevance to the majority of homeless and near homeless in the area. It is also the only one not centrally located. All things distasteful to commerce are located there. These currently include the Hunger and Health Coalition, the Community Cares Clinic, and a satellite program of Caldwell Community College and Technical Institute. Proximate to one side of the cluster is a combination of trailer parks most commonly known as Bradford Park. On another is GDS Waste Disposal Service. Just up the street are the McLeod Center – a methadone clinic, [19] and Rock Haven. Not far away are a rock quarry and a local landfill. Hospitality House and the WeCAN program will round out the services located there when relocation is complete late in 2010.

Several changes inherent in serving the homeless and high-risk individuals in Watauga will be set in motion by the relocation of the shelter. First, on the positive side, many in Bradford Park have long suffered from a lack of connectivity to basic services. Hunger Coalition offered a connection to basic preventive needs such as food, and medications, along with whatever finds its way into the donation closet for others to reclaim. Hospitality House will allow many of those struggling with temporary shelter among friends to again improve their access to stability through service coordination and referral.

Unfortunately, some of them will take the easy way out and acquire shelter through one of the new beds formed in the expansion. The new shelter may fill up quickly with people who could make a better choice. Despite such potential, the shelter will be able to relax into fully meeting people's needs for awhile, instead of pushing guests to make connections and get out.

There is a bus stop located just outside of the front door, which has generally facilitated the Coalition and CCC&TI's needs quite well. The shelter will have somewhat different access hours in the realm of employment. Getting to Able Body to seek day labor will be impossible, and many working late will have to find creative ways to get home. Since the bus runs differently when the campus is closed or between sessions, such clients will have to be made aware of the changes before their jobs become endangered. Several transportation options may be pursued to overcome this obstacle, including acquiring a company van, or pleading for a route schedule change with AppalCart. At least the route is one of the more consistently available ones year round.

---

[19] Although there are some shared clientele, the McLeod Center staff corroborates my own observations that the incidence is extremely low. The treatment tends to be cost-prohibitive in the long-term. Methadone treatment locally tends to be accessed long-term.

Inside the town of Boone is where most of the changes will occur. Commerce is supportive of the move for two reasons: (1) the moves of Hunger Coalition and OASIS really did not cause much of a stir. OASIS did not move far, and the Coalition operates primarily during routine business hours. (2) There is a perception that the move will facilitate commerce by making the street crowd disappear. In 1984, the perception was virtually the same, except the idea was that the shelter would give them a place to go. But, most of the street crowd is not homeless. Many of them want to be where the action is, and some of them, like the businesses they hang out near, want to increase their potential customer base, whether they are selling stones, songs, sketches, or less legal things.

The street crowd did not disappear in 1985, and it will not disappear now. There is some potential that it will increase to include more homeless – at least until each one learns where the shelter is, and how to get to it. If the businesses do not make a point of remembering, and downtown remains primarily full of non-locals, gaining such insight could take awhile. Also, those who do not qualify for shelter services will not waste time going to it in the first place.

The soup kitchen at the shelter also enjoyed a brisk business. It did so for two reasons: (1) people need to eat, and it offered a divergence from the equation *no money = no food*; and (2) people enjoy company. The soup kitchen moving away from downtown will remove a social aspect for the impoverished that live there. Most of them will not see an hour or more on the bus round-trip as an acceptable cost to gaining the camaraderie if they can come up with any other option for food, including not paying their electric bill, and asking for help with it later. An alternative will have to emerge.

Several potential options exist: Food Not Bombs has regularly tried to establish a permanent chapter in Boone; various churches have employed Loaves and Fishes type programs in many other towns; and, Salvation Army has offered soup kitchens in many places as well, so I am sure one or more replacements will emerge. First Presbyterian has offered community meals in the past, as has First Baptist. Living Water currently offers a regular community meal, and Shelter Rock prefers aid missions that do not require those who come to disclose their level of need. Several other churches with community focus round out the set of potential responses.

Watauga Conclusions

The heart of homeless service provision in Watauga County has resided in the community almost since the County's beginning. As in most rural areas, in the absence of shelter, families and friends in Watauga have taken steps to care for loved ones, sometimes needing and utilizing outdoor aid. This practice continues through the present day, although outdoor relief is now a collection of targeted community and governmental programs. Unfortunately, some individuals have always managed to slip through cracks in their social networks which creates the demand for public shelter.

Most common among that group in Watauga have been single individuals who just could not manage a household by themselves. In recent record, finances and addictive behaviors have been the catalysts for such lack of housing, although among women, domestic violence has been the primary reason presented for a number of years. In the time of the County Home, such factors were not as clear, but singles were already prevalent.

After services form and lose a bit of their luster, their trend in the county seems to be to grow more and more dependent on outside guidance and aid. This is partly a factor of allowing those things peripheral to one's own life to slip into the shadows. Conjoined with this is that, when too few are trying to do too much, those things with the most support are the easiest to pursue. At the core of the trend is simply that there is not enough fiscal reserve in the community to support agencies year-round. Those with the fiscal capabilities to offer such support are targeted so heavily during their brief stays that many of them are discouraged from forming local social networks inclusive of the permanent population.

Overarching those trends is a persistent cycle among different levels of governments. Solutions are developed at a local level, or adopted locally by modifying examples found elsewhere. When they are successful, they become more commonly implemented, and become supervised by progressively higher levels of government. As supervision climbs, so do the ranks from which finances are expected to be received. Oversight remains necessary at each preceding level. Such oversight becomes expensive to require, and funds are restricted. As funds become restricted, programs are compartmentalized. That is, they cater to the most common, or the least contested, sub-categories among the homeless population. The combination both reduces efficacy by presuming only a small variety of causes for homelessness, and increases required justification by increasing the number of distinct reports required to receive adequate funds, at least in areas that do not have a large enough population for agencies to specialize. Such a cycle expedited the destruction of the County home model, and led to Deinstitutionalization.

The current situation has settled into a nationally compartmentalized stage. I.e. oversight, fiscal aid, and acceptable recipient categories are all defined and directed at the federal level. Government funding comes primarily from federal tax dollars; and, the homeless receiving aid are expected to fit neatly into the categories currently defined. This has not really threatened the existence of Watauga's services yet because each agency seeks to provide as many opportunities as possible for their guests. Competition for outside resources, compartmentalized or not, is still locally minimal, so budgets are cobbled together from a variety of grants added together to meet the maximum of needs with a minimum of budget. Much like the lives of those depending on welfare, the cost of such practices is an increase in administrative time spent on justifying and tracking a multitude of programs, which requires either more staff to accomplish the agency's goals, or less time spent with those receiving the services. Because maintaining continued eligibility at the same level requires that all grant funds must be spent within the grant year, services are frequently provided to clients just because they can be used. This often divides the beneficiary client's focus from achieving stability towards achieving comfort. The system is unsustainable on all levels.

The city of Boone is growing. As it becomes urban, more programs are required, and more individuals require each program. Two of the most recent programs covered by this research have formed for essentially the same purpose: WeCAN and Salvation Army both offer crisis assistance programs. There has already been some redirection of resources as the Salvation Army was formerly a donor of WeCAN. This mild competition is most likely only the beginning.

Other changes may be on the way. The relocation of Hospitality House's Bread of Life Meal program outside of town limits threatens to require the creation of another soup kitchen, which is likely to compete for resources with both the shelter and the food pantry. Similarly, as affordable housing becomes increasingly scarce, the waiting list for Section 8 rent subsidies is going to grow longer, both in numbers, and in length of time it takes to receive a voucher for subsidy. Increasing numbers of individuals will not be able to maintain safe alternatives without becoming homeless, and more of their families will be stretched too thin to help without the danger of falling into the same trap. Already, the majority of the NRHA client base is single women, many with dependent children. Thus, if urbanization continues, and it most likely will, the numbers of women requesting shelter will increase. Since they do not currently prefer the services of Hospitality House, the issues involved will become more apparent and a separate shelter for women and/or families will likely have to evolve, posing competition for both Hospitality House and OASIS for locally based resources.

Although it will not necessarily help diversify funding sources, or reduce administrative time spent in justification, one solution is to expand the local CoC by courting unattached Caldwell County allowing additional funds to be spread over the district's programming. Increasing the membership base attending those meetings might allow an increase in resources simply by drawing in new ideas and sectors of the community. Building the new shelter on a foundation that supports upward growth could also ease the potential burden by allowing a second or even third story to increase the serving potential when the time comes to again address increased demand.

The county has done a lot to assist its populace over the years. With the services polarizing into various centers around town, the potential exists for a lot of targeted corroboration to improve and stabilize those services, but care must be taken to keep them all working together. If that does not happen, given the urbanizing trends at work in the county, the services will all begin to drift apart, and necessary competition for resources as new services emerge will create conflicts than can be avoided.

Of course, being an election year, changes in presidential and congressional administration could mean significant changes in the way federally granted funds are dispersed, as well as how much funding is available. The way current grants are designed, a significant increase in available funding is likely to translate into an increase in numbers of programs instead of increased stability for existing programs. New programs in Watauga usually are picked up by existing agencies, along with yet another series of reports necessary to maintain those grants each year. When such increases are followed by decreases, programs may disappear, along with service jobs, or all programs may suffer cuts that the agency cannot compensate for locally.

When such decreases are concurrent, programs and agencies are severely jeopardized. Appalachian shelters, already surrounded by less affluent communities, suffer more than the larger, tradition-defining urban shelters that have more diverse and stable community bases. Although Watauga's agencies will all likely survive the current round of changes, regardless of direction, tightening of their budgets would promote emerging conflicts caused by an increasing number of agencies competing for limited resources.

CHAPTER IV

THE APPALACHIAN COMPARISON

As stated in the introduction, there is no single representation of homeless service provision in Appalachia. Each community response is distinctive, largely due to the social and historical conditions around which it was formed. The limited comparisons I have been able to make during this research have suggested that local community action in Appalachia, regardless of how each community has manifested, has been at the forefront of developing services for its homeless. Federal and state governments have usually become involved later in providing structure and guidance whether it was needed or not. It was primarily when those governments got involved with budgets that they became cumbersome to work with, especially when they were providing funds for which they wanted to prove themselves good stewards.

When contemplating patterns of homelessness in Appalachia, we must remember that America was settled and formed to satisfy the early global marketplace, and used to alleviate a variety of strained social conditions existent in communities left behind. Demands for resources exceeded the supply throughout Europe; and, the pressure was on to find a means to provide for a growing population. Methods for dealing with those least capable of competing were also much in demand. The melting pot that America became for its first centuries provided an outlet for both those who were seeking opportunity – whether as investor or as laborer, and those for whom successful integration into society was not likely at home.

The area now called Appalachia was long at center stage for that agglomerated marketplace, both as a set of geologically formed obstacles impeding the exploration of the continent, and as a huge resource bank, full of timber, hides, a variety of ores and minerals, and a wide uncivilized area in which to test a variety of emerging transportation technologies. For those whose ambitions did not reach so far, the opportunity also existed for homesteading.

Gary Nash (2004) found that during the seventeenth and eighteenth centuries, roughly ¾ of those who arrived in this country arrived as slaves and ⅔ of the remainder arrived as indentured servants. The result is that over 90% of the settlers during that time arrived without the opportunity to acquire land. By the time those individuals had earned or bought their freedom, land was in short supply, even if it was mostly uninhabited. Tenancy was the best for which most could hope. J.P. Arthur (1915/1976) noted much the same beginnings for Watauga's early settlers.

Comprised of both the dispossessed and the dispossessor, most of America's settlers would have been well-versed in the existing methods of coping with the less fortunate. These were essentially almshouses, work-houses, or in the worst areas and times, forced expulsion from the city (Foucault, 1965). Land ownership was the number one way to ensure that one's family would not easily go without.

Given Nash's research, it is clear that such opportunity was only readily available to about ten percent of the early American population, and almost exclusively to those who were among the wealthier classes in Europe prior to their arrival. Many of those wealthy landowners remained at home, acquiring land in the New World as investors only, a situation Appalachia continues to experience today with both corporate and private absentee landownership and, increasingly, seasonal homeowners and national franchises as well. Opportunity only decreased for those who came later to work in mines and on the railways (Westview Special Studies, 1981). The potential for equality was a dream unlikely to expand into economic standing from the start.

The Emerging Record of Appalachian Homelessness

I found no research available on homelessness specific to the Appalachian region as a whole, but there are a few sources refering to various localities or institutions. Many agencies have some sort of documentation of their own history available to those who request it. Local newspapers often cover the issues faced by the local homeless and the agencies that serve them. County records buried in the North Carolina State Archives also give a quantity of information related to various time periods.

Conrad Ostwalt, Jr. (1992) found a recognized desire to care for Black orphans at the dawn of the twentieth century. In 1901, Presbyterian and Mennonite missionaries opened a Black orphanage in Elk Park, NC despite earlier resistance of the local citizenry to the development of a Black school. Continued racism, among other concerns, unfortunately, led to the home's closure in 1912, but the continued activities of the Mennonite missionaries would eventually result in the development of Black Mennonite churches throughout western North Carolina, including the notable one in Boone's Junaluska Community.

Similar acts of mission work to alleviate poverty and other perceived social maladies occurred throughout Appalachia. After William Goodell Frost began identifying the region as Appalachia in the late nineteenth century as a means to garner investors in Berea College and its projects, external interest in philanthropic opportunities exploded and many such activities began all over Appalachia (Munn, 1965).

Reverend John C. Patty (1914), in compiling the biography of Reverend Lucius Bunyun Compton, describes that clergyman's response to a need for a home for battered women and an orphanage during the same time period. Additionally, the church practice of Reverend Compton near Asheville, NC gave him the opportunity to open Faith Cottage, a home for "wayward women," when a young woman in his congregation professed the desire to leave her life of adultery if only she had somewhere else to go. Faith Cottage was soon followed by Eliada Orphanage in 1907 (Patty, 1914). From the various State Biennial Charities Reports, it is clear that Compton's Faith Cottage and Eliada Orphanage were kept current of state requirements, even seeking licensure early on when many were actively avoiding doing so. Grandfather Home also opened during the early twentieth century in Banner Elk, NC to serve as a region-wide orphanage (NCSBoPC, 1915). Unlike the Elk Park orphanage discussed by Ostwalt, all three of these last organizations can still be seen today.

From survey returns produced by my research, it is known that Salvation Army began operating urban ministries in what would become Appalachia at least as early as 1852. Those same results demonstrate that the wave of emerging shelters beginning in the 1970s and peaking in the mid 1980s were as often as not born of concerns raised by local pastors and congregations. Many of the services I observed through site visits and the survey of shelter providers cited direct activity of church coalitions as key to their foundation. Other factions of community also pursued similar humanitarian activity, especially post-Deinstitutionalization.

Survey Data Analysis

In early spring of 2006, I mailed a survey to 185 agencies offering shelter services in at least one Appalachian community. I requested demographics and other data related to their agencies and their 2005 program years. A follow up was made to those for whom an e-mail address or fax number had been found. Of those, there were only 18 comparable responses, a rate of just under 10%. Not all respondents answered or demonstrated understanding of every question.

Those 18 came from 17 different Appalachian counties in five different states. Two from Georgia and four each came from Tennessee, West Virginia, Ohio and North Carolina. The dual county response was from Tennessee. Those 17 communities appear to serve specifically at least 50 different Appalachian counties. Less definitive responses, such as the "north West Virginia Panhandle" or even more simply "the southeast," expand the overall service area. Thus, a roughly 10% return rate from the states offering respondents serves over 12% of the total Appalachian region's counties.

The survey itself was divided into six different sections designed to capture information useful for two disparate purposes. The abandoned first purpose was to create a database of Appalachian shelters for their own networking needs. The second and more important purpose for this thesis was to collect comparative demographics on the homeless in order to gain insight into when, where, how, and why shelters began throughout the region.

Agency information section.

Section one asked for general non mission specific information respective to each agency. As a rule, all responses demonstrated understanding of this section. The section concluded with several questions aimed at the formation history of each agency. Some of the earliest formed shelters did not list their incorporation dates, but those that did demonstrate that early shelters took the longest to pursue such recognition. Seventy-five percent of responses indicating a start before 1970 were Salvation Army shelters, the remaining 25% were Young Women's Christian Association (YWCA).

Most of the later shelters sought incorporation either concurrent to opening their doors, or succeeded in incorporating within their first couple years. Incorporation became more important throughout the 1980s to the point that all but one of respondents opening post 1990 were founded and incorporated in the same year. From survey data, Watauga appears to be the only provider who became incorporated prior to offering services. From personal knowledge and the agency's internally recorded history, I know that the coalition of churches that formed the shelter was providing skeletal shelter services in anticipation of the building to be acquired and renovated (Hospitality House, 2005). I found this to be indicative of the increasing importance placed on governmental recognition the incorporation process.

Only the Salvation Army shelters reported that they used the non-profit fiscal year as once set from October to September, with the remainder of respondents demonstrating only a slight preference for the calendar year over the governmental fiscal year. That none took advantage of the option to set an alternate fiscal year implies that all were looking outside their own communities for example, guidance and aid. That none followed the example of the Salvation Army suggests that national charitable organizations were not high-priority examples for contemporary shelter models.

Since the time of the survey, Watauga has changed its fiscal year to match the governmental one in order to more efficiently match the primary sources of its funds. If none of the other respondents has done the same, this affects an equal split in the trends afforded by calendar versus governmental fiscal representation. The primary benefit of the fiscal method is to equalize reporting years for agencies requiring an audit as more and more dependence and accountability to government agencies becomes the norm. Such synchronicity frees up more time for implementing the program by reducing the time spent in tracking various sets of the same demographics and justifications.

The size of area served by each respondent was usually cited along county lines. Three counties served was by far the most prominent catchment area, being both a clear norm as well as the median size. My time as Program Director of the Volunteer Outreach Center (VOC) suggests that is not uncommon.[20] North Carolina and Tennessee proved the least concerned with state lines in determining whom they served. They also offered most of the larger catchment areas. The respondent from Forsyth County, NC, cited service to the entire southeastern United States. Ohio demonstrated a preference for single county services, and provided all of the single county examples.

In regards to the oldest shelters, it is likely that the multi-county service areas were resultant from a combination of the early twentieth century push to form multi-county contracts as aging facilities became expensive to maintain and the long-time tendency of less affluent

---

[20] Quite a number of the 125 local nonprofit and human service agencies and civic groups listed in the VOC database stated a similar service area, including the High Country United Way (HCUW). For many agencies, catchment size was a factor of matching the HCUW, serving Ashe, Avery & Watauga Counties, who was often the biggest potential financial supporter for less marketable agencies.

communities to look to the commercial centers near them to offer aid. That several states looked favorably on county homes adopting the trend offered both example and encouragement to do the same.

One of the largest clearly defined catchment areas is that of Hospitality House of Boone, which officially serves the same seven county area designated by North Carolina as Region D. Region D is a recognized local development district (LDD) adopted by a variety of governmental organizations including the Appalachian Regional Commission (ARC), the NC Department of Administration (NCDA), HUD, and the OEO (Bradshaw, 2002; High Country Council, 2008; Local Development, n. d.). Development efforts are coordinated in the region by the High Country Council of Governments or the Northwest Continuum of Care. That the official catchment area is based more on politics and economics becomes clear when one looks at the areas from which guests present for shelter.

Neighboring Caldwell County, currently outside any Continuum's oversight, contributes several guests each year but is not part of the Hospitality House's catchment. From informal talks with HUD staff, I know that the city of Lenoir is designated as an entitlement zone, which means that any Continuum its county joined would qualify for additional funds beyond what the county itself qualified for. Caldwell has successfully maintained programs for domestic violence and alcoholism, but has not consistently or yet successfully maintained an emergency shelter. According to the Caldwell County Sherriff's Department (personal communication, Fall 2007), the last short-lived attempt at running such a facility resulted in the donated property being redirected to the domestic violence program circa 2005, when the fledgling program collapsed. Although it would increase required accountability and community organization, creating or joining an existing Continuum of Care would allow ear-marked funds to become available.

Father Blanck, now pasturing a church in Sparta, observes that service providers in more distant Alleghany County currently do not realize a need for shelter, even though 10% of its residency requires the preventive measures offered by a local food pantry. Since almost no homeless originating in Alleghany present to the regional shelter in Watauga County, it appears that their local evaluation is still accurate. Alleghany is claimed to be part of Hospitality House's catchment area, despite an absence of client traffic.

Wilkes County has long had a general shelter that opts not to pursue federal aid. A permanent supportive housing program called Wintergreen started in 2004 does receive federal funds. NRHA oversees Wintergreen directly. Although Wilkes has local shelter, the county contributes regularly to the sheltered populace of Watauga. The most common client profiles experienced during my employment at the shelter were former addicts trying to break free from an unhealthy social circle, and families who felt insecure in their local shelter. Although Wilkes can and largely does provide necessary services for its own, it is part of the Watauga-based catchment area.

Program information section.

This very short section asked agencies to identify their distinctive programs, who they served, and the nature of their occupation of the properties they utilize. Forty-four percent of respondents were organized as domestic violence shelters, although 88% reported that they readily assisted that population. Nearly half (44% each) agreed that they served families, single women, and the general homeless. Thirty-eight percent reported continuing assistance available for those transitioning out of homeless situations, while only 25% reported the ability to offer assistance to those who were in danger of becoming homeless. Both outreach and follow-up have proven to be an integral part of crisis recovery, not only in addressing homelessness, but also in addressing mental health, substance abuse, and just coping with short term disasters (Erikson, 1976).

Fifty percent of survey respondents cited community planning in the creation of their shelters. That number is increased to 67% if you adjust it for Salvation Army's tendency to work with local ministries in identifying needed services. Half of the resultant set was distinctly faith-based in their genesis. Fully two-thirds (69%) of survey responders owned their own properties. Twenty-five percent each leased and/or received donations of property use for their missions. Donated space was always office space provided by a church.

Services offered section.

When it came to services offered, things became a bit more complex among such a small sample. Most facilities, as expected, accepted a variety of ways for clients to access their services. Walking through the door or referral by a community partner were the most common responses. Some, especially DV shelters, used hotlines, while introduction through local law enforcement remained a less common option. No methods were offered that were not suggested examples on the questionnaire.

The average daily occupancy (ADO) of reporting agencies ranged from one to only thirty-three. No single program reported in the sample averaged more than seventeen, even in larger Appalachian cities. The mean and median ADO were both nine individuals. Despite the prevalence in federal jargon of the term bed-night, very few responders adequately answered the question related to annual bed-nights to draw any usable data. Ideally, the annual bed-nights would be roughly equal to the ADO times the number of days a shelter was open during a given year. It was surprising that even the larger urban shelters that answered cited low ADO. Although several respondents did not submit an answer, it was clear that Appalachian shelters remain small.

The American Red Cross shelter in Tompkins County, New York was not sent a survey, but during visits to the shelter, it was observed that it tracked its annual bed-nights both with and without hotel assistance, because the true ADO was significantly larger than available space. It is probable that some responding providers made, but did not offer up, this distinction. Benefits observed in this method of tracking included the ability to lobby the various segments of the community for specific types of aid and to regularly evaluate how efficiently both hotel funds and shelter space were being applied. John Ward, the shelter's director is cited in the local papers as suggesting that the shelter was much more effectively used than hotels (Geismar, 2007). This shelter is discussed at greater length later in this chapter.

Just over 50% of respondents routinely dealt with an excess of demands on their available bed space. Referrals to other shelters, making room, and purchase of hotel stays were the normal ways of handling the situation. Only those who stated that demand never exceeded availability cited turning the client away as a method of response.

Interestingly, no respondent charged the clients for services, regardless of length of stay. This surprised me in that I have known of several non-Appalachian urban ministries that charge daily or at least weekly for their services. The reason cited for such charges has always been to force guests to find work. Although it was not anticipated by the survey, I suspect that the ready availability of day labor opportunities will prove significant to this Appalachian peculiarity.

When asked about average length of stay, agency responses ranged from one night (in a hotel) to one year. Thirty days was both the norm and the median length of stay (25%) reported. All of those reporting an average stay of 30 days offered a maximum stay of 90 days.

The program reporting a one-year average was a transitional program offering up to two years. One shelter offering a maximum stay of 30 days reported an average stay of 45 days. A similar problem caused Hospitality House in Watauga to reevaluate maximum lengths of stay in 2002, when it was realized that guests were averaging 70 days. The determination was to allow 90 days with more thorough monthly client progress evaluations.

The last question asked in the services section of the survey was a straightforward request to check off which services were offered, and write in others as necessary. Virtually all write-in responses matched options already listed. Not surprisingly, 88% of the sample offered general case management and crisis intervention, 81% offered housing referrals and meals to their guests, 69% offered outreach, access to local transportation options, laundry, showers, and clothing dispensation and/or referrals. Fifty-six percent were able to provide hygiene items, direct transportation, and employment referrals. All other services among the 39 listed choices were provided by less than 45% of agencies.

Old debts not posing a direct obstacle to setting up a new home, move in expenses, and homeless prevention assistance were each offered by 25% of respondents. Surprisingly, since only 13% listed a significant number of other organizations offering services in their area, only 19% of agencies offered a soup kitchen. Six percent of respondents did not answer the question at all. A significant portion of the respondents (31 – 44%) also offered education, relocation and life skills training.

Among the items listed, the only two options that no one chose were "legal dispute settlement," and "HIV/AIDS related services." The Point in Time Survey completed in January 2007 for the Region D area of North Carolina listed 19 individuals (1.8%) among its 1,069 identifiable homeless in the region who were in need of HIV or AIDS related support. Only one of those individuals accessed shelter and identified that need at Hospitality House between 2005 and 2007 (Mason, personal communication, 2008).

"Food pantry" was unfortunately absent from my list, and no one wrote in the option. Since shelters in all three communities visited during the course of this research offer food assistance, I must also suspect that many of the respondents do. The Watauga shelter supplements the local food pantry's efforts when there is surplus donation beyond the needs of the residency and soup kitchen. The Red Cross shelter in Tompkins County, New York participates in an active pantry system, accessible from multiple locations (J. Ward, June, 2006). Likewise, the REACH program in Washington County, Maryland provided food assistance.

Persons served section.
The persons served section of the survey was the most difficult from which to glean usable data from the available sample. This section requested the total number of individuals served and a breakdown by such factors as age, race, gender, and presented problems. So few responded adequately to each question (and some did not respond at all) that most of the results gleaned are speculative at best. It was clear, however, that race and ethnicity are not distinguishable to many providers region-wide. Unsurprisingly, Whites comprised the largest racial component among the homeless reported. Blacks bring up a distant second and Native Americans bring up a still more distant third. Hispanics and Asians also showed up in small numbers, even in the larger cities.

Out of only 40 identified homeless Native Americans, 73% were in Greenbrier County, WV, and 18% were in Watauga County, NC. Eighty-six percent of Blacks were located in Forsyth County, NC, and almost all of the rest resided in larger cities. Also unsurprisingly, Hispanics were noted in the majority of responses. The largest concentration (40% of 79 total) was also in Forsyth County.

Employment status was reported on only 1,129 (35%) of 3,200 identified homeless. Of those, 28% were employed full time when they entered shelter. Almost 59% were unemployed. One shelter housing 420 guests during the year claimed 100% unemployment at entry, which skews the results towards high. Less than 2% were declared unemployable. Roughly 10% were employed part time, while less than 3% had already started a training program.

The normative annual number of persons accepted into a program was 100, although the mean was 117 and the median was 248. All shelters accepting families included minors in their total counts, but only one respondent appears to have been able to accept them unaccompanied by a parent.

Lastly, only 55% reported on veteran status. Of these, 50% recorded no veteran stays, and the remaining 50% reported a total of 160 male and 5 female veterans. Eighty-one percent of these were sheltered in North Carolina in either Forsyth (58%) or Watauga (22%) counties. The third highest group (18%) was in Coffee, TN. The remainder was divided between two shelters in West Virginia. West Virginia appears to be more attractive to female veterans than elsewhere in Appalachia, but with only five women counted, the numbers are hardly conclusive.

Budgets, staffs and community partners section.
The final section was related to what resources were locally available to perform the agencies' missions. Since money can be a touchy subject and I wanted at least some data, I asked respondents to identify into which range their staff sizes and budgets fell. I also asked agencies to identify if there were other agencies performing related functions in their localities. (See Table 4.1)

The smallest 19% of staffs enjoyed a budget of less than $50,000 a year, while the largest 19% had budgets between $.5 – 1 million a year. The second lowest 19% had budgets less than $250,000, while the remaining 31% operated on less than $.5 million. From a conversation with Jennifer Herman of OASIS (2006), I am aware that their budget also fell into this last category. Twelve percent did not respond to this question.

Table 4.1: *Survey Ranges in Budget and Staff Sizes*

Annual Budgets		Staff Size (FTEs)	
19%	less than $50,000	31%	0-2 Full Time Equivalencies
19%	50,001 - 250,000	12%	3 - 5
31%	250,001 - 500,000	25%	6 - 10
19%	500,001 - 1 million	19%	11 - 20
-	more than 1 million	-	more than 20

Note on Abbreviation: FTE = Full-time equivalency

As expected, staff sizes climbed directly in relation to budget. Again, 12% abstained from responding. There was a slight lag between a rise in budget and a rise in staff. Thirty-one percent had two or less full time equivalent paid positions (FTEs).[21] An additional 12% had five or fewer FTEs, while 25% more kept their FTEs under ten. Only 19% had more than ten FTEs, and none had more than twenty.

Two-thirds of those within the largest staff brackets were located in the counties with the largest 2000 census populations among the survey respondents. Additionally, the two largest shelters by numbers served – Kanawha County, WV (Charleston) and Forsyth County, NC (Winston-Salem) – each listed 3-5 other providers in their vicinities.

Problems experienced in the survey.

Terms that have made it into the canon of homelessness language still do not have the same interpretations everywhere, especially those promoted by federal and state agencies among agencies who do not receive funding from those sources. The provision of a list of definitions with the survey did little to standardize usage of those terms within survey answers. Several questions were rendered less useful for this fact. The term "domestic violence" has become so successfully integrated as a buzzword that I erringly offered it on the list of choices for three different questions. This made it easy for respondents to choose the most common definer of their mission, although not necessarily the most appropriate response to provide the information the question at hand sought to interpret.

There was also significant confusion between the terms "crisis" and "emergency." Crisis shelters are a common part of community emergency plans. They are opened up for short term situations affecting unusual amounts of people and offer a safe place to wait for other programs, such as FEMA, to be able to re-house them. Such communal response could be resultant from a natural flood, a forest fire, or larger disasters like Buffalo Creek's 1972 mining disaster (Erikson, 1976), and the more recent Hurricane Katrina in late 2005. Emergency shelters, in contrast, are generally open all the time to standard victims of homelessness. They are also likely to become full in the event of a crisis, but operate by a standard set of guidelines at least seasonally, but more often year round.

I administered the survey during a time when many of those agencies for whom it would have been the easiest to complete were in the process of preparing requests to continue to receive funding from

---

[21] Respondents were not asked to declare their definition of full time. It was taken for granted that forty hours a week would be unanimous and that many providers would work above the hours for which they were officially paid.

HUD and OEO. Some of them, especially in the southern part of Appalachia, may also have been dealing with the confusion that came along with working with Katrina victims, most of whom had been given the impression that returning home was imminent. Several willing agencies responded with apologies and a pledge to respond later or next time. Shelters not seeking federal funding may not have tracked such data, and, therefore, had no easy way to respond thoroughly.

Population Analysis of Survey Respondents

One of the themes I looked more closely at within this research was the distinction between provision in urban and rural areas. That provision methodology is nationally guided by urban principles remains without doubt, and that rural communities retained more heart in services provided is likewise upheld. I wanted to know what else could be seen. As previously discussed, this research distinguishes urban and rural based on a population breakpoint of 50,000 as evaluated along county lines.

Mid-census population estimates were calculated for counties responding to the survey based on a consistent rate of growth between the two nearest decennial censes with a preference towards large round numbers. Although they are reasonable approximations for this research, growth is not always constant and such numbers should not automatically be taken as adequate for all research. A database of decennial censes for each Appalachian county was compiled for the years 1900 – 2000 in order to provide all such populations and calculated estimates in this chapter, except where otherwise noted (U.S. Bureau of the Census, 1995a; USA Counties, 2002).

Some cities and towns arguably reach urban status before the counties that host them due to their status as economic centers for the surrounding region. Rural shelter services, when offered, usually develop in such urban centers and reach beyond county lines. Thereby, individual services within a town – whether you consider outlet malls, electric companies, sheriffs' offices, shelters, or crisis hotlines – if considered based on the populations from which their clients will consistently be allowed to present, could be classified as urban even sooner than the cities that host them. The majority of shelters responding to the survey could be considered accordingly.

For example, Hospitality House of Boone in Watauga County, North Carolina officially serves the seven North Carolina counties referred to as Region D. Region D had a population of 194,016 at the time of the 2000 census. Only Wilkes County had a population base larger than that of Watauga in the region. It also has its own shelter. I know from my employment at Hospitality House that the active catchment area at the time of the census comprised five North Carolina counties, totaling 227,293 citizens and two Tennessee counties with a combined population of 74,241. The active catchment area, with 301,534 residents, contained three urban counties, including one with its own shelter. The active catchment area also contributes significant numbers of employees to Watauga's businesses.

The only responding shelters serving one county only were all in urban Ohio counties. The other respondents reporting less than three counties served were both in Sullivan County, Tennessee, which has been urban by the current standards since circa 1930. Thus, Appalachian rural areas clearly maintain larger catchments. As a town becomes viewed as an urban center, it begins to serve the less fortunate of the surrounding areas until it can no longer support its own needy efficiently. As the surrounding areas also develop, they develop their own services, and catchment areas dwindle while demands rise. As more shelters develop in a county or city, some of them will specialize their services, some will streamline their process, and some will no longer distinguish between local and transient, serving all comers.

All of the responding shelters formed before 1970 were created in urban areas by nationally recognized non-governmental organizations, usually by the Salvation Army, but with the exception of the response from Ohio County, West Virginia, which was founded by the YWCA in 1906. When that sheltered opened, differentiation of state institutions into a variety of categories, ranging from race and gender to physical and mental infirmities, was common and gaining momentum. It had further become known in many areas that not all who became homeless were transient men, a fact that would gain increasingly more light during both world wars as well as the great depression (Tollett, 1992). The overall urban picture of respondents demonstrated a median county population of 115,400. The mean population was 66,000, with a norm essentially the same. The median date of foundation was 1957, which is in the middle of a 35-year period with no noted shelter formations. The mean foundation was 1980, with a normative range centered only a year higher.

With but a couple of exceptions in the largest cities, those shelters formed after 1970 were in the more developed rural areas. The exceptions were additional shelter programs in areas experiencing a homeless population outgrowing the previous infrastructure. Beginning in 1987, the size of communities beginning to offer shelter programs became noticeably smaller than in prior years. Among rural respondents to the survey, the median, mean, AND norm for foundation was 1987. Coincidental to that time, the Reagan Presidential Administration had recently slashed HUD's housing assistance funding by over 70% and the Stewart B. McKinney Act had begun the testing of a variety of programs targeting the less fortunate in response to national outcry around homelessness and mental health reform.

The average county population demonstrated by the survey for pre-1987 rural shelter start-ups was 33,000. From 1987 to 1995, that average dropped to just short of 17,000. The mean and median of all rural responses was roughly 24,000 with no clear norm. Although increasing mobility undoubtedly encouraged facilities to centralize local regional services, the potential for federal aid was also a likely trigger for beginning to provide needed programs.

When looking at all responses, the overall picture represented by this data comparison is less clearly definable. The median inception date for all respondents was 1962, while the median county size was 58,000. Again, the year misses all responses by over a decade. It also includes communities that already had at least one shelter in place when the responding shelter began. The mean data falls on 1981-2 with a range in the mid-thirty-some thousands. This is only slightly earlier and more populous than expected, despite larger urban outliers to skew the data. That rural shelters more commonly responded probably corrects part of the offset, as does the obvious fact that urban areas did not stop forming new shelters when rural shelters began to appear. The overall norm is more intuitive than obvious, since there was very little duplication of data response. A true norm of 1987 is still observable, although that year more truly falls at the end of the densest normal range. The most common range of populations within which shelters formed was 20,000 – 27,000.

I call the overall norms intuitive because the data set is not large enough to differentiate definitively rural and urban trends. The patterns are too distinctive not to mutually skew the true picture. It is reasonable that the first shelters were community founded and located in urban areas. Without a large population, community contributions alone could not support such a venture, especially when those same areas offered fewer capital-based opportunities and values. Appalachia, having been settled primarily by those who were capable of working with and subsisting off the land, focused more on developing community rather than market interconnectedness.

As global trends fluctuated, communities in the region were content to provide abundant resources in exchange for making local subsistence efforts more efficient, and livelihood more healthful. All of this is true of most rural areas settled during national expansion, but the diversity of ideas and skills being developed and explored while the Appalachian Mountains were being breached left it with a deeper and broader spectrum of knowledge than later settlement communities. The time afforded as westward expansion continued to the west coast, and before the resultant backflow of population, allowed that knowledge base to settle into the regional culture recognized on various fronts during the twentieth century.

Denser populations allow interactions among and with the less fortunate to be more publicly visible, allowing an increase in both public awareness – positive or negative, and private detachment. County homes were also still a publicly available option in many areas between the mid-nineteenth and mid-twentieth century, which provided a publicly available option funded completely by local tax structures. In the United States, early cities formed primarily for political or commercial reasons, facilitating linkages to colonial governments, national and international trade routes, or specific resource extraction and/or production. Such purposes also allowed the variety of global welfare concepts to be vetted and implemented before they had been fine-tuned to successful programs.

Ultimately, after populations nationwide had settled and established local identities, the diversity of US citizens began to emerge. The mid-1960s featured the War on Poverty, recognition of Appalachia as an impoverished region, and the formation of the Appalachian Regional Commission (ARC). One of ARC's foci is towards enabling Appalachian communities to come up with ways to increase their local connections to the national economy. This was done through the local development districts, as described earlier. It was presumed that such districts would allow poverty-stricken areas to conform to national economic standards while maintaining their local flavors.

The 1970s was a time when federal and state institutions were disbanding in an effort to honor personal rights to self-determination. The right to remain in the stable care of a specialized institution despite other shortcomings was not among those perceived. This required the development of community out-patient treatment programs and the absorption of self-insufficient individuals back into family folds or low-budget single-occupancy housing units, which often made use of housing subsidies, where and when they were available. Such encouragement promoted community awareness of a variety of case-types, including mentally, emotionally, and physically disabling ones caused or exacerbated by the traumas of the Vietnam Conflict.

Such awareness included responses of compassion, frustration, anger, and exploitation. Ultimately this led to conditions in the 1980s, when everything came to a head under a presidential administration that focused on the national and corporate economy with almost complete disregard for individual economy alongside the promotion of decentralized exploration of methods of care-giving. Housing prices rose as programs fluctuated. Cost of living rose as incomes diverged. Thousands barely scraping by found their support networks unraveled while communities explored options for providing aid to those whose situations were still but poorly understood and inconsistently evaluated.

The removal of established federal, state, and regional safety nets forced communities to feel once again the needs of their own citizens, and left those communities no choice but to respond accordingly. Therefore, communities of moderate means- i.e. sufficient population base – began to implement the options demonstrated to them at the time when the demand was growing most obvious. It can be no surprise that most of the shelters responding to the survey were opened between 1979 and 1992. The federal government began to offer homelessness funds later in the decade as those shelters continued to struggle. The aims of programs guided by those funds are largely directed by the conditions experienced just outside the doors of congress, a reality not indicative of conditions for homeless in most of America.

The 1980s is clearly the time when demand was growing in many areas. Eight years of Reagan and a strong international economy meant things were not going to improve any time soon for marginal populations. A county population around twenty thousand is emerging as an expectable population base needed to make shelter-based services nominally successful. Watauga County had roughly this size of a permanent population when its shelters first began forming. It is ironic that Appalachian shelters tend to become regional in nature, although local funding comes primarily from the host community. If all communities in a catchment area would get on board financially, a shelter could be established much earlier without as much need for federal support. Unfortunately, NIMBY[22] policies emerge when too many location options are identified as potential options.

A glance at just North Carolina respondents demonstrates a potential hypothesis that shelters formed over time in direct relation to population. The responses in this subset were 100% from most to least population over time. None of the other states supported that brief hypothesis, however. In addition, West Virginia presented almost exclusively urban responses, and none that were founded after 1979. Tennessee, on the other hand, presented only one response founded before 1980, and included the most recently formed respondent, founded in 1999. Its exception was a Salvation Army shelter opened in 1865.

The data collected offers a range of foundation dates from 1852 to 1999 with concurrent county populations from 14,500 to 246,000. Excluding Tennessee, there is a vague but expectable trend of formation dates progressing from north to south within Appalachia. Eighteen percent of respondents did not share their year of foundation. Of those that did, 64% were rural and 36% were urban. One of the urban counties offered two responders and one of the rural counties was transitioning to an urban status. Fourteen percent of responses were from counties already over 100,000 when the shelter was formed. At the time of the 2000 census, the 17 host counties were divided at 59% rural and 41% urban. Nearly 18% of the shelters were on the verge of reclassification as urban. Eighteen percent of counties were above the 100,000 population mark in the year 2000.

North Carolina in Appalachia

Since the primary research site for this thesis was Watauga County, and much of the local historical data for that county was either destroyed by court house fires or archived in the state's records, archives, and universities, quite a number of sources found dealt with issues from the state perspective. This section will discuss information gleaned for North Carolina Appalachian communities, as well as some of the various linkages between the state and national trends that were called into play.

Central to the state's treatment of those found homeless was the segregation of different sets of marginalized citizenry from within the County Homes and other almshouses in the state. Most differentiation was either social – such as Confederate Widows, or clearly related to

---

[22] "Not in my back yard."

physical health – such as blindness, and met with little resistance. The status of orphan invoked enough sympathy and concern that orphanages and group foster homes likewise met with little resistance. Two primary areas of segregation met with contention: race, and mental health.

For the most part, emerging policy handled race with the same muddled logic and blinders as it always had been. County homes across the state had separated both gender and race in separate wings or buildings to the best of their ability from the start, mostly with the aims of minimizing sexual threat to women and maximizing the pretense of superiority among Whites. Appalachian North Carolina was overwhelmingly White outside of the densest urban areas and former plantation areas. Rural areas such as Watauga did not seem to notice any racial distinction, at least on paper, among paupers who were Black or White, although non-pauperized minorities appear to have remained in neighborhoods comprised largely of single races (Ostwalt, 1992).

Mental health was a separate issue altogether. Up until World War I, there was no true distinction between mental health and physical health in the United States (Brown, 1928). Various methods of control and aid had been employed throughout the centuries, all based on segregation and physical and dietary treatments (Foucault, 1965). By the start of the twentieth century, feeble mindedness was the diagnosis of choice for paupers in Appalachian states, attributed variably or in combination to inferior stock, poor education standards, and inbreeding among various groups of people or localities. Various missions were being plied throughout Appalachia to rectify such social faults by well meaning, but frequently misguided missionaries.

A quotation from Dr. E. B. Sherlock (1911) sums up the understanding of treating mental illness of the day:

> Since no two cases of feeblemindedness are alike, the making of a classification involves the acceptance of certain conventions. There must be agreement as to the respects in which likeness exists, and as to the degree of likeness, in any particular respect, which is to be regarded as constituting similarity. Classification is akin to the formation of concepts. Its aim is to render a mass of facts more easily handled by substituting one for many, and its utility will depend on the amount of information which the type form supplies as to the characteristics of the group for which it stands. (p. 180)

From Sherlock's text, it is clear that the process of understanding mental health as a separate field was just beginning, and that the focus was not yet on making things easier for the afflicted individual, but on making the process efficient for the one rendering diagnosis. Perhaps it should have been obvious that it was a bit pre-mature of government bodies to rush out and build specialized state institutions for the care of such patients. Hindsight, as they say, is 20/20, and the pitfalls of rushed institutionalization prove no exception. A study of early public institutions found that although they were "[o]pened in a blush of Progressive Era optimism over the efficacy of institutionalization, these facilities gradually devolved into custodial warehouses where maintenance rather than training became the watchword [by 1940]" (Noll, 1995, p. 155). Steven Noll went on to find that the States creating these institutions generally left them to flounder in the need to focus most of their efforts on justifying their own existence and funds rather than their original missions. Southern states in particular seemed to jump on the poorly executed examples set by their northern neighbors as if they would solve all of their social problems.

Foreshadowing what was to come, Sherlock, in developing his poorly executed example, states, "An incomplete census, taken by investigators equipped with different standards of what constitutes "mental defect" will not, in the nature of things, give entirely trustworthy results. This is not for our present purpose, a matter of great consequence" (Sherlock, p. 262). Although a 1922 census of county and state institutions was in many ways quite complete, two very different individuals, utilizing two very different perspectives on reality, conducted the inspections (Brown, 1924).

Although it remains true to its own posit that "The undesirable elements of society, the delinquent, the defective and the dependent, are parasites--voluntary or involuntary--on the body social and politic." (NCSBoC&PW , 1922/2003, p. 10), the 1922 Board of Public Charities Report remains one of the best sets of data collected for county home demographics in North Carolina. In addition to demographics on and visits to all of the county homes, a number of additional studies were conducted.

The State Board was intent at the time on proving that those receiving public aid outside of state institutions were all mentally deficient on some level. Towards this end, they surveyed eight shelters across the state giving those inmates who were home mental examinations. The only Appalachian county surveyed happens to have been Watauga County, where thirteen individuals received testing. Of those thirteen, nine (69%) proved to be feeble minded, two (15%) proved to be mentally abnormal in an unclear design, one test was inconclusive and only one (8%) proved to be normal.

For those in North Carolina's total county home sampling of 126 individuals, 68 (54%) were feeble minded, eighteen (14%) were abnormal, seventeen (13%) were insane, fifteen could not be properly tested, two were epileptic, one was a drug addict, and five (4%) lucky individuals were confirmed as normal. It is more than clear that the Board found exactly what they were looking for in the qualitative arena. The quantitative data (Table 4.2), taken directly from that same document in electronic format (NCSBoC&PW, 1922/2003), proved a bit more utilitarian. It must be noted that the University of North Carolina at Chapel Hill has property rights of the electronic version of said report, and has made it freely available for research, teaching, and personal purposes, so long as a statement to this effect is made.

The quantitative data collected is useful in evaluating primarily gender and race compositions, but it also offers some clue as to familial patterns. It is immediately noticeable that Blacks are frequently absent from the record. Only one-third of NC's 30 Appalachian counties currently had Black inmates, and four of those ten counties had only one in residence. The two counties with the largest black populations were Forsythe (44%) and Buncombe (19%). Those same counties were the only ones in Appalachia to offer boarding homes for Blacks at the time Watauga converted its Home nearly a quarter of a century later.

Stokes County, the northeastern most of NC's Appalachian counties was the only county to shelter more Blacks than Whites (6:5). Geographically, both Stokes and Forsythe to its South, are in the most populous portion of Appalachian North Carolina, and lay in the foothills, where the agricultural industry could still operate on a large scale. Forsythe's responses to the mailed survey previously discussed, indicated the presence of 86% of the Blacks documented in that survey. In 1922, they claimed only 45.3%. Forsythe and Stokes counties together sheltered 62.3% of those recorded in NC Appalachia in 1922.

Region-wide, the breakdown of inmate races suggested by the 1922 study provides only 12.2% Blacks and 87.8% Whites. For the sake of curiosity, Appalachia without Forsythe and Stokes drops dramatically, to only 5.8% Blacks. On the other hand, North Carolina as a whole is seeing a rate of 30.2% Blacks, which compares to a rate of 35.9% in 1911 (NCSBoPC, 1912).

It would not be until the early 1930s that North Carolina would realize that there were more than two races using the Homes. Two non-

Table 4.2: *Reported Appalachian County Home Populations in North Carolina: 1922*

County	Males Wh	Males Bl	Females Wh	Females Bl	Normal Wh	Normal Bl	Feeble minded Wh	Feeble minded Bl	Married Couples Wh	Married Couples Bl	Widowed Male Wh	Widowed Male Bl	Widowed Female Wh	Widowed Female Bl	County Calcs
Alexander	6	1	7						1				2		14
Alleghany	2		3										1		5
Ashe	5	1	6				2				2		2		14
Avery	3		3								1		1		6
Buncombe	10	4	15	5	2		2	1	3	2	3		2	2	39
Burke	8	1	8	1			5		1	1	1	1			23
Caldwell	5		8								1		3		13
Cherokee	1		4				1				2		1		6
Clay															0
Davie	2		6										2		8
Forsyth	14	16	20	8					1		4		4		58
Graham															0
Haywood	12		16				4		1		4		3		32
Henderson	3		2		1										6
Jackson	3		2								3		2		5
McDowell	2	1	4		1				1		1				8
Macon	3		6										2		9
Madison	7		10						1		2		5		17
Mitchell	3		2		2								1		7
Polk															0
Rutherford	14		18	1			2		4		3		4	1	35
Stokes	3	4	2	2									2		11
Surry	11		15		1				1				8		27
Swain	3		5						1				1		8
Transylvania			6										2		6
Watauga	4		12				4				1		4		20
Wilkes	9		23				1		1		1		3		33
Wilson		2	8	3								1	1	2	13
Yadkin	3	2	8	1	1						2		3		15
Yancey	1		2								1				3
App Calcs	137	32	221	21	8	0	21	1	16	3	29	5	59	5	441
NC Calcs	447	280	649	205	28	5	29	17	41	10	107	63	192	52	1648

All data with the exception of calculations: North Carolina State Board of Charities and Public Welfare, 1922/2003.

Notes on abbreviations: Wh = White; Bl = Black; calcs = calculations.

Appalachian counties were discovered to have included Native Americans in their reports designated as White (NCSBoC&PW, 1934). The clues were there at least as early as 1911, when 40 individuals were included in reported totals without a race noted (NCSBoPC, 1912).

Gender is a bit more straightforward. In 1922, two genders only were universally recognized. Not surprisingly, in the wake of World War I, there were more adult women than adult men staying in the Homes. In Appalachia, there were nearly 59% women, while in North Carolina, as a whole, the rate was only 56%. Watauga County was much higher at 75% women.

Women were more likely than men to have become widowed, but in such close proximity to war, the variance was surprisingly small among this population. In Homes in Appalachia, 26% of women and 20% of men were surviving a spouse, roughly 3% lower than in North Carolina as a whole. One third of Wataugan women and one fourth of the men were surviving a spouse, both higher than the state average. It was far less common for married couples to find themselves at the Home with 9% of Wataugan and 6.4% of North Carolinian inmates married. Obviously, the loss of a spouse is a contributing factor for both genders where need to seek sheltered support is concerned, but the absence of a spouse altogether is a much more common occurrence.

A first glance suggests that Blacks showed up much less frequently in conjugal states, but the difference between Black and White marriages is only 3% in Appalachia as compared to 7% statewide. Roughly 2/3 of inmates in either race have never been married. Although economic indicators in the 21st century commonly point to the need for two incomes to maintain a household, the presence of over 90% unattached individuals among the shelter population suggests that two adults have been needed to maintain a household for a lot longer than economics has required it. Although the mailed survey did not adequately collect such data, the 2005 – 2007 Hospitality House fiscal years cited 12% of individuals in the emergency shelter with families; and, most of those were single parent households.

Children do not appear in large numbers in the county home data in North Carolina. At the strong suggestion of the state, once they were deemed old enough to separate from their mothers, they were generally sent to relatives, orphanages or boarding schools. Grandfather Orphan's Home, which began serving the surrounding region from Banner Elk in

1914, often cited children in residence who still had one or even both parents living.[23] The request for pauper funds by parents for their own children under outdoor relief is also not uncommon (Watauga County Registrar, 1960; NC Clerk of Court, 1969; North Carolina Department of Archives and History, 1969).

In 1922, only 6.8% of Appalachian inmates were children, as compared to 3.9% in North Carolina. This suggests that Appalachians were somewhat less inclined to be pressed into separating families. Even Buncombe County, which maintained a variety of specialized regional facilities, did not remove all children from the poorhouse environment. Although we cannot tell the ages of children from the data, the notation of "under 16" suggests that they are not all infants in the care of a parent. In 1922, there was only one Black child sheltered in all of NC Appalachia and there were only seven total in state as a whole. Although this fact appears to support the probability that Black children were more likely to be separated from their families at this time, there were too few such families to make such a claim with confidence based on the data. It would be more reasonable to say that Blacks were discouraged from seeking such help in some way.

As part of the press to empty the Homes, children were more often than not to be designated as feeble minded. Within just a couple of years after this report was published, part of the outdoor aid roster as well as the press to send children of poor homes to orphanages would be replaced by a program called Mothers' Aid (NCSBoC&PW, 1922/2003). This new program would also take some of the burden off counties to provide 100% of assistance by providing matching funds from state and federal coffers. As program recipients were no longer becoming or remaining homeless, that program has not been followed by this research, despite its preventive attributes. The 1922 report declares that Mothers' Aid was begun and initially financed by various local churches. It had gained enough interest by the time of the report that a bill had been introduced to render it governmentally promoted (NCSBoC&PW, 1922/2003).

In the following pages, I will provide comparisons of data sets gleaned from a variety of sources, including my homeless provider survey, Mance's ten-year study, annual report demographics filed by Hospitality

---

[23] By 1936 Grandfather Home had space for a maximum of 86 children but ultimately sheltered 103 children in that same year. Of those 103, 63 were girls. Additionally, 59 of the total were there due to the death of only one parent, and 19 were qualified even though both parents still lived (NCSBoC&PW, 1938).

Table 4.3: *Gender and Shelter Population in Appalachia*

	ADO	singles			# fams	Adults in families			children			total served		
		M	F	T		M	F	T	M	F	T	M	F	T
HH-ESG 04-05	14	132	35	167	20	9	20	29	13	4	17	154	59	213
HH-ESG 05-06	16	147	39	186	15	9	14	23	10	6	16	166	59	225
HH-ESG 06-07	17	158	39	197	12	12	11	23	7	1	8	177	51	228
2007 Region D PIT	1069	732	112	844	160	28	76	104			121	760*	188*	1069
OASIS 2005													53	53
HH-94-05												1080	420	1500
2005 Survey Appalachia	129+													3716
1939 NC-Appalachia PIT	639				-	-	-	-						
1922 NC-Appalachia PIT	441	169	242	411	-	-	-	-			30	169*	242*	441
1922 Watauga PIT	20	4	12	16	-	-	-	-			4	4*	12*	16

Sources: Hospitality House Emergency Shelter Grant Report from fiscal years 2004-5, 2005-6, & 2006-7 & the 2007 Region D Point in Time Count (Mason, personal communication, 2008)
2005 OASIS data (Herman, personal communication, 2006)
Hospitality House 1994-2004 data (Mance, 2005)
1922 Point in Time Counts (NCSBoC&PW, 1922/2003)
1939 Point in Time Count (NCSBoC&PW , 1939)
The 2005 Appalachian Survey is part of this research.
        Notes on abbreviations: ADO = Average Daily Occupancy; M = Male; F = Female; T = Total; fams = families.

House of Boone, the 2007 point in time survey for Region D, and 1922 and 1939 data by the various NC charitable oversight Boards.

Table 4.3 analyzes populations in Appalachia by gender and age states. It is clear that the male to female ratio among those seeking general shelter has undergone a reversal in Appalachian North Carolina since 1922, a trend that is particularly obvious in Watauga County. This is not surprising in that during the earlier period the nation was just recently out of World War I. A study of homeless veterans found that the draft tended to be particularly heavy on the less affluent segments of the population because they had fewer opportunities to beg out of service (Tollett, 1992). Appalachian poverty is well noted.

Two methods for tracking presented problems emerge from the data. The first method documents only the primary problem, while the second method captures all shared obstacles to regaining stability. The ten-year summary by Mance and the 2007 regional Point in Time data collected by the Northwest Continuum of Care, using the second method, total more presented problems than the total number of homeless, while most of the other data sets, using the first method, suggest clients faced only one obstacle. The 2005 survey summarizes less than the total homeless due to inconsistencies of reporting among respondents. Additionally, changes in what was tracked over time render the 1922 data and the ten-year summary incompatible. Nevertheless, there are some things extractable from the complete set. (See Table 4.4.) Domestic violence is a reason for homelessness for roughly half of those currently identified as homeless regionally.

We observe that mental illness, drug abuse and dual diagnosis have been rising in Watauga County. The data captured by the Region D point in time survey supports the conclusion that the trend extends into Appalachia, at least within the confines of North Carolina. In regards to the survey, respondents generally had trouble with this question, except for DV shelters, which existed for those primarily displaced by domestic violence. However, one specialized shelter does shed some light on alcoholism in particular. One responding shelter is able to house unattended children, and cited the presence of over 900 children of alcoholics during the year. Clearly, alcohol abuse is still an active part of our society, and an active contributor to homelessness populations. Although alcoholism in Watauga appears to be in decline, it is a likely byproduct of increased prioritization of limited bed-space combined with an increase in the dual diagnosis nomenclature. Thus, alcoholism did not

Table 4.4: *Presented Triggers for Homelessness in Appalachia*

Reason for Homelessness

	MI	Alc	Dr	DD	DV	Un	Und	Ev	Pr	Tr	Rel	Dis	Total Served
HH-ESG 04-05	14	28	7	41	10	22	7	18	15	14	27	5	213
HH-ESG 05-06	21	21	11	46	14	15	14	22	21	6	17	16	225
HH-ESG 06-07	32	18	37	89	6	15	2	1	19	6		3	228
2007 Region D PIT	283	518		-	514								1069
OASIS 2005					53								53
2005 Survey Appalachia	15	60	49	10	1885			3			22		3716
HH-94-05	224	500	302		109	1086							441
1922 Watauga PIT	0	0	0	0									13

Note: Abbreviations are as follows: mental illness (MI), alcoholism (Alc), drug abuse (Dr),

dual diagnosis of MI and either Alc or Dr (DD), unemployment (Un), underemployment (Und),

eviction (Ev), release from prison (Pr), transience (Tr), relocation (Rel), and disability (Dis).

suddenly become less common; alcoholics were just declared mentally ill and/ or denied service.

There are several other ways in which people can be marginalized by their communities. Table 4.5 looks at a few of these, namely race, ethnicity, and veteran status. As in the other tables, the survey captured incomplete data, although veteran status and race received clear responses. Ethnicity is not generally well understood by either service providers or the homeless themselves. Most of the general population just treats it as an extension of race, and that was clear in the details. In the 1922 samples, everything was simply viewed in terms of "Black" and "White," North Carolina having only recently switched the choices from the more inclusive "Colored" and "White."

Table 4.5: *Veteran Status, Race, and Ethnicity Among Appalachian Homeless*

	Veteran		Race/Ethnicity						total served
	M	F	As	Bl	Wh	Hi	N.Am	BiR	
HH-ESG 04-05	32	2	0	12	184	5	6	6	213
HH-ESG 05-06	21	0	1	19	186	3	10	5	224
HH-ESG 06-07	25	1	0	6	198	6	5	3	228
2005 Appalachia Survey	160	5	2	641	2405	88	45	7	3716
1922 NC-Appalachia PIT	-	-		54	387				441
1922 Watauga PIT	-	-		0	16				16

Sources: Hospitality House Emergency Shelter Grant Report from fiscal years 2004-5, 2005-6, & 2006-7 & the 2007 Region D Point in Time Count (Mason, personal communication, 2008)
Hospitality House 1994-2004 data (Mance, 2005)
1922 Point in Time Count (NCSBoC&PW, 1922/2003)
The 2005 Appalachian Survey is part of this research.
Notes on abbreviations: M = Male; F = Female; As = Asian; Bl = Black; Wh = White; Hi = Hispanic; N.Am = Native American; BiR = Biracial.

Veterans in the Appalachian shelter system are hard to come by and have generally settled in regions surrounding a Veteran's Administration (VA) Hospital. In recent years, those services appear to have become more difficult to access, or at least more of the cost is passed on to the patient. A commonly perceived reason for this is that a rise in illegal immigrants is causing a drastic increase in access to services that are then never paid for (Woodring, personal communication, 2008). No VAs were captured during this research, so this research cannot corroborate the extent to which that has become reality. The conjunction of VAs and homeless vets obviates that health issues are a common contributing reason for veteran homelessness.

The reported upon veterans were overwhelmingly in North Carolina (81%), and almost all in Forsythe County (58%) or Watauga County (22%). The State of North Carolina was operating a variety of Veterans' Homes during the early 1900s. The majority of Veterans unable to return to families or maintain their own homes would have been sent to one of these, which would account for the lack of available early data. Incidentally, there is no VA in Watauga. Guests of the shelter needing VA services travel to the next county over in Tennessee, or an hour south to Hickory. The presence of options made Watauga a desirable compromise between larger urban areas.

Appalachian inmate populations in the NC County Homes in 1922 had a ratio of 88% White and 12% Black. In 2005 Appalachia, according to my survey and adjusting for the 528 for whom race and ethnicity were not noted, the population had evolved to 75.4% White, 20.1% Black, 2.8% Hispanic, 1.4% Native American, and 1.7% mixed or other races.

This number may be misleading in that only 28.6% of the urban areas that responded reported on the breakdown of races. If the remainder is adjusted to demonstrate the rural areas only, the figures become much starker in contrast. We are left with a 91.1% White population, salted with only 3.9% Black, 2.5% Hispanic, 2.1% Native American, and only .4% mixed or other races. The scant urban response provides a breakdown of 55.7% White, 40.4% Black, 3.0% Hispanic, 0.6% Native American, and 0.1% Asian population.

In general, it is the White and Black segments of the population that seek shelter in Appalachia. Others are either of too low a population to show up significantly, or else simply avail themselves less of the system. Native Americans aside, it would appear that length of establishment within the nation plays the most significant role on access. If you consider that Native Americans were largely driven out of the region, then the same could hold true for those entering into the region to resettle on ancestral lands where there is as yet no upholding community to offer a social support network and reassert the former connection.

Northern Appalachia

Two communities outside of North Carolina were visited. Two visits were made to Tompkins County, New York, and one was made to Washington County, Maryland. The first New York visit was in June of 2006. The second New York visit and the Maryland visit were in May of

2008. As my visit to Maryland was brief, I will treat it first within this narrative.

Just as a group of churches had joined together in Watauga county to form a variety of homeless and near homeless services over the years, Religious Effort to Assist and Care for the Homeless (REACH) was formed in Hagerstown, MD (Washington County) in 1990 (Schotz, 2007). REACH originally offered cold weather shelter aid through area hotels, but in 1996, various churches began offering nightly shelter via stints of two-week rotations until Christ Reformed Church was able to purchase and renovate an old shoe factory on Franklin Street. Now the location stays the same, but the churches continue to provide meals and volunteers at the shelter in rotation (Washington Square, 2007).

Tina Barse and Jill Parker in an unscheduled interview (May, 2008), shared that REACH also currently hosts a day shelter, open until one in the afternoon, formed partly to address the tendency for many homeless to use the public library as if it were designed as such a facility. REACH provides preventive measures – such as crisis assistance, and volunteer care – such as transport to doctor appointments, grocery shopping, and light housework (Washington Square, 2007).

Despite the assertion by one City Councilmember that providing shelter invites homelessness, the bulk of REACH's direct fiscal budget currently comes from the city of Hagersville. The largest charge to the bequest is for paid security, which cannot be performed by volunteers for liability reasons. Volunteers provide the majority of additional staffing. REACH, whose shelter mission is primarily for the protection of life, is the only shelter among several in Hagerstown that does not currently require at least a 30 day county residency in order to qualify for stays. Its primary requirements are a willingness to respect house rules and be an adult. Families with children are helped through area hotels if another shelter cannot be found. This minimizes many potential risk factors of working with a diverse and sometimes transient population.

Washington County is experiencing growth in its homeless population both from internal and external sources. Housing costs are still high, despite a slump in the housing market that leaves many houses unsold; but, unemployment is low and low-wage jobs are readily available. The roughly two year waiting list for Section 8 housing choice vouchers actually attracts regional homeless who compare it to nearby Baltimore, where the wait is for up to three years and jobs are less abundant (Barse & Parker, personal communication, 2008).

REACH sheltered an average of 54 people per night for a total of

8034 bed-nights in the 07/08 season, beginning on October 28, 2007 (Schotz, 2007). They served 276 (81.9%) different males and 61 (18.1%) different females. When the shelter closed down for the spring, it continued offering crisis intervention services on alternating days with shower and laundry services two days a week each. Additionally, at the time of my visit, REACH had already scheduled half of their volunteer nights for the following season (Barse & Parker, 2008).

The ability to plan volunteer commitments ahead may prove to be a saving grace since food pantry requests are up across the region (Associated Press, 2008; C. Fortuna, personal communication, May, 2008; Henbest, 2008). The call was already out for volunteers to provide lunch for the next season before the summer was well underway (Herald Mail Staff, 2008). Since income generated by local housing sales provides the funds from which the city dedicates its support, continued support for the 2008-2009 winter season is still uncertain and likely to remain so well into the new year (Barse & Parker, 2008).

The American Red Cross shelter in Ithaca, New York (Tompkins County) is directed by John Ward, who was kind enough to give me two separate interviews and allow me to access his staff for tours of his emergency shelter and the Friendship Center, a day shelter open to those who may not be able to utilize traditional shelter, either because of lifestyle choices, or lack of space available. Many such individuals live by choice in a nearby homeless community known as "the Jungle" (Brown, 2001; Geismar, 2007; Getman, 2007). The facility also offers a food pantry to anyone who might need it and mail service to those who do not have a permanent address.

Ward (personal communication, April, 2006) has found that the Tompkins County Shelter is one of only about six shelters maintained by the Red Cross nationwide. They are not all in Appalachia. Walking through the front doors of the Red Cross offices results in an immediate blaze of activity confronting the senses, as the variety of health and safety concerns pursued by the staff catches your eye. The building is an old renovated house, much as Hospitality House in Watauga is, and the architecture still shows it off as such. I had to keep reminding myself that the majority of staff there was not working with homelessness issues.

As indicated in the chapter on methods, there were some similarities in the way the shelter system in Ithaca and that in Boone were organized, especially in regards to my own philosophies, which I did not initially share with my hosts. Much as mandated behavioral healthcare changes had brought about the creation of OASIS in Watauga

County, mandated social services programming began what grew into the Tompkins County homeless program. The Department of Social Services (DSS) began helping individuals through local hotels in 1983 until they could enlist additional aid.

Ward shared that the initial request for aid led to the opening of a six-bed shelter in the unfortunate position above a restaurant and bar. Although we did not discuss the ramifications of the placement during our interview, I could not help but think of the Sleeping Place located across the street from not one, but two restaurant bars. The presence of vigilant staff went a long way towards curbing temptations.

Ward began working at the shelter in 1994, which then had 25 emergency shelter beds and 18 transitional shelter beds dispersed between three locations. A comparatively low census, followed by budgetary adjustments soon led the agency to consolidate into the location I visited in 2006. Consolidation eliminated all of their transitional programming as well as a lease on an extra building.

As fate would have it, a year later they were again utilizing hotel space, and after two years they were offering nearly the same number of beds in hotels as they were in the shelter (Ward, 2006). Now, ten years later, they are looking at renovating the Friendship Center into additional shelter space that will create an additional 18 beds (Geismar, 2007).

According to Ward (May, 2008) space may begin to be utilized by winter 2008, but the primary goal is to see the renovations done correctly from the start. The current Friendship Center programs will move to the back of the building. The new shelter will take over the vacated space while also occupying the second and third floors. The plans include facilities for onsite supervision and a limited number of transitional style beds operating in conjunction with other local programs.

The emergency shelter currently offers only 13 beds in a community with 18.1% of the population living below the poverty line (Geismar, 2007). Geismar cited 13,439 bed-nights of shelter in 2006, providing an average of 37 people per day with shelter through those thirteen beds and hotel stays. In the 2000/2001 fiscal year, the bed-night count was only 8199, comprising 669 adults and 176 dependants (Brown, 2001) for an average of 22.5 sheltered guests per day. Diane Hardy, who was the Director at that time, observed that "Homelessness is on the rise" (Brown, 2001). Time certainly proved her observation accurate.

Although compassion and second chances are always available, according to Ward he shelter is a short-term solution focused on getting people into stable housing. Guests are not allowed to enter intoxicated, and may be required to get a substance abuse assessment if it seems necessary to facilitate continuance in the program. Guests are asked to leave their belongings bundled, so that if situations change and they cannot make it back into the house, their bed can simply be "rolled up" to make room for another to use. Towards achieving the goal of a rapid transition back into housing, Ward recognizes that a shelter needs to be a place of security and comfort but its guests should not be able to get too comfortable in their temporary surroundings. In speaking to the need for additional beds, he is quoted as saying "People in motels think that they are motel guests and not shelter clients. We need them to think like they are shelter clients. We need them feeling the urgency every morning that it is a short term shelter" (Geismar, 2007).

In 2006, Ward was quoted as saying, "We take an holistic approach. We know that when someone comes through our door, the fact that he is homeless is just the tip of the iceberg. Something in that person's life has led him to this point" (Brown, 2001). It was clear to me rather quickly that this agency was trying to strike a balanced approach to addressing homelessness. Their Continuum of Care is comprised of members from a larger group called the Homeless and Housing Taskforce, which is itself comprised of 40-50 individuals from local housing agencies. The local DSS, having birthed the program in 1983 is still involved to the point of weekly meetings with shelter staff.

A bonus is that DSS, the Friendship Center, the ARC shelter and offices, access to potential jobs, residences, and several helping ministries, are all within a few blocks of each other. The benefits of the ability to walk to appointments during such a time in a person's life became doubly obvious when I attempted to access the local bus service. The bus I accessed exists primarily for the benefit of University students, but just crossing the Cornell campus cost over two dollars. It charged based on the zone system. If a person in danger of homelessness needed to depend on this service to make his or her appointments scattered around town, s/he would hasten the process of becoming homeless tremendously.

I first visited the Friendship Center in 2006, on the same afternoon I first visited the shelter. It is officially closed to those in the shelter between 9am and 3pm, although no visible sign of the enforcement process was obvious. Several folks were sitting out back when I pulled into the tiny lot, reminiscent of that behind Watauga's emergency shelter and soup kitchen. In fact, the Friendship Center does provide some meals and a food pantry for shelter guests and those who are not yet ready to access shelter. The pantry system in Tompkins County is not consolidated. It provides 14 different access points throughout the county, several of which can be accessed 24-hours a day (Ward, personal communication, 2006; Tompkins Pantry Directors, personal communication, May, 2008).

The facility was not crowded, and I observed a man who knew he was not in an appropriate state to come in. He stepped to the door to politely call the attendant, and then retreated down to the sidewalk. She went out and spoke to him a minute, retrieved his mail and a cup of coffee and he quietly went on his way. When Ward arrived with supplies for the pantry, most of which were purchased, several individuals proceeded to help unload his car and put them away.

The diversity of missions was obvious in the Red Cross offices, as was it clear that this required a much larger staff and budget. I did not inquire as to how large the budget for homeless services was, but it did appear that attachment to a nationally recognized crisis agency afforded at least a level of stability to the operations side of working with the homeless. The idea was not pursued, so if that stability was actual, or was of a similar nature to that claimed by federal support agencies remains unknown.

As I was fortunate enough to have a wonderful friend in Ithaca performing a residency at Cornell University's Veterinary department, I explored Cornell University's library, which was of primary benefit for a few general titles I was able to glean for future request. The Cornell archives were not centrally located as Appalachian State University's are. In fact, they were divided among several locations around campus, part of which only provide documents with prior request. The few I was able to request during that first visit have been determined inconsequential to this research. That the University was involved in the process of creating the existing homeless service infrastructure could be seen from the record, and a program running from 1987-1996 under the School of Hotel Administration seemed particularly interesting for its scope. The "Housing and Feeding the Homeless Program" appears to have been active in some form from 1981 to 1996, with classes running until the present. The program involved coursework, research, and implementation of programming (Housing and Feeding, 2005). The latter entailed targeted work of a nature similar to that of intensive service learning or internships. After returning home from my first visit to Tompkins County, New York, I learned of some changes happening in the community and additional programs of interest to this thesis. I also wanted to revisit the Cornell library archives. John Ward was still the program's Director, Crystal G. was still running the drop in center – soon to house more bed space and several offices for guest service coordination, and Kim was still keeping everyone straight at the shelter itself.

I consulted neighbors who told me that the closest thing to trouble they experienced with the shelter nearby was the occasional apple core tossed over the fence into their garden and occasional request to recycle cans or bottles.[24] Neither situation was necessarily due specifically to shelter proximity.

Although there was not a scheduled CoC meeting during my travels, John Ward was kind enough to invite me to a meeting of the Tompkins County Food Distribution Network, attended by representatives from the area food pantries. The meeting agenda that month was loosely organized, so I was able to give a quick presentation on the Hunger and Health Coalition in Boone, North Carolina. Several found the differences interesting and asked a variety of mutually enlightening questions.

I also visited Tompkins Community Action (TCA), the local Housing Authority, where I visited one of the food pantry locations while collecting data from Danielle Harrington, the agency's Director. Although small compared to Hunger Coalition, the pantry was well organized, very clean, and strove to meet the needs of its prospective clientele, including some consideration of alternative dietary needs, and basic off-the-shelf medications. It suffered some from the reduced availability of TEFAP,[25] but still made effective and efficient use of that program and Second Harvest Food Bank in general.

In addition to Section 8 voucher assistance, then being provided with temporary abundance and minimal waiting periods, TCA also facilitates the local Head Start Program, two group home programs, and assorted energy and weatherization programs.

A visit to the local Salvation Army confirmed that it does not

---

[24] In New York, cans and bottles have a deposit associated with them, so they are rarely seen for long along the roadside. The recycling of them can be a lucrative business for an industrious individual. In North Carolina, there is no such deposit value, so quite a few are needed to make their salvage pay off.

[25] The Emergency Food Assistance Program utilizes staple-type foods provided through the U. S. Department of Agriculture (USDA). An increasing demand for products by public schools (due to a growing population) combined with reduced domestic farmlands and restricted budget keep availability lower than in previous years.

offer shelter in Tompkins County, but does offer another food pantry, and a weekend meal program targeting the two days a week when Loaves and Fishes is not offering a community meal. There was quite a crowd gathered for assistance during my visit.

Lastly, I stopped in at The Learning Web, which offers assorted programs for youth, including a Homeless Youth Outreach Program. Operating a variety of programs in two locations, I was never able to catch either director in the office. The outreach offices especially were hard to access staff. On two separate visits, I never found a single staff person, but I was able to see a wonderful collection of resources posted prominently to assist even semi-motivated youth in finding their way forward. The agency was seeking a candidate for the homeless outreach coordinator position during my visit, accounting for the lack of access to thinly stretched directorial staff. The secretary in the central office was able to give me several informative reports demonstrating the variety of program accomplishments.

Since the program began, Learning Web has assisted over 2000 homeless youth between the ages of 16-25. A 2007 Independent Living Survey compiled data from 204 individuals, or roughly 1/3 of the contemporary homeless youth in the county. In the community at large, males only slightly outnumber females, contrary to national statistics (U. S. Census Bureau, 2006). Among the homeless youth, there is an even greater, but relatively slight tendency towards males (The Learning Web, 2007). The variance is too slight to base assumptions without more precise age and gender demographics for the agency.

The clientele is equally divided between those who have and have not reached their 21st birthday (The Learning Web, 2007). Racially, whites form the majority among homeless youth (The Learning Web, 2007), but they are significantly underrepresented compared to county demographics (U. S. Census Bureau, 2006). It is significant to note that despite a significant and growing Asian population in Ithaca, none appears among the homeless youth (U. S. Census Bureau, 2000; U. S. Census Bureau, 2006; The Learning Web, 2007).

Active familial relations and expectations (e.g. conflict, turned 18, thrown out) were by far the top reasons kids found themselves homeless, while the absence of access to familial relations (e.g. dead, jailed, absent) placed near the bottom of the list. Despite a significant percentage of young parents, the presence of a child was at the very bottom of the list of why kids were without home.

Not too surprisingly, familiarity with "the system," with

weapons, and with a variety of abused substances was common. Cigarettes, marijuana, and alcohol were overwhelmingly the top three, with significantly more experimentation among the younger half of the sample.

The most significant obstacle emerging for youngsters in the study was competing for jobs in a community that boasted a high rate of high school graduation and three active college campuses. Successful apprenticeship and mentoring programs offered by the Learning Web attest that this is also a problem faced by many youth who do not come to experience homelessness.

New York's Historical Record.

I accessed some historical record discussing those poor houses that once existed in New York. In 1856, the last of New York's Appalachian Counties had recently been formed, and still depended upon its counties of formation to care for those who once fell into their districts. A systematic inspection of all of New York's Homes at the time ranged in onsite population from 30 – 86 inmates despite claimed averages from 35 – 130 at any given time. In most cases, the average reported was higher than that experienced by inspectors. Tompkins County had 37 out of 53 (69.8%) documented inmates at home. The Keeper was among those away. Appalachian counties presented 714 in residence of an expectable total of 896 (79.7%) inmates, while New York as a whole presented 4,956 of 6,420 (77.2%) (New York State Select Committee, 1857/1976).

The reason for such a low percentage found at home is not clarified. It may be that some could work and were off doing so, or that there was a significant fluctuation between births, deaths, intakes and discharges. It appears more likely that there was little attempt to temper a consistently high rate of "intemperance," that is, alcoholism, among guests, and that inebriates were simply out pursuing their vices. Alcoholism was presented as the reason for pauperism of 68% of contemporary inmates in Tompkins and Appalachia, and 69% statewide (NY State Select Committee, 1857/1976).

The report continues to disclose that 24% of those in Tompkins County were children as compared to 19% in Appalachia and 28% statewide. Low mental functions (lunacy and idiocy) were the secondary reason at 17% in the county and state as compared to 20% in Appalachian counties. Sensory impairments (blindness or deaf mutes) were a distant third at only 0.4% in Appalachia and 1.5% in the state.

There were no such individuals in Tompkins County (NY State Select Committee, 1857/1976).

The second set of data uncovered was from 1822, being compiled by the Secretary of New York State as a report in 1824 (Yates, 1824/1971). This volume was a singularly complete piece of work demonstrating an honest desire to come to terms with what was seen as a statewide problem. Although the biases and aspirations of the compilers were but softly masked, no other report uncovered by this research has been so complete in its scope. It even outstrips the 1922 North Carolina State report previously discussed.

Data were collected for the report not only from New York's various towns and counties, but example was also collected and presented from a variety of States and even other countries, often citing a letter of request for information (Yates, 1824/1971). There is little doubt that the original report has been an example to future states beginning to organize their efforts towards charitable and penal institutions.

The primary problem emerging in the report is the seeming liberties it has taken where math is concerned. As with the North Carolina reports, there are instances of what could have been transcription error, or even outright guessing of a local number not reported but estimable from past report trends. In the case of this document, data were gleaned largely on a town-by-town level, with examples from almost every county being garnered. Many towns failed to provide statistics for any number of unknown reasons. By some unclear method, the compilers of the report determined that the reported numbers of paupers were only inclusive of 63% of the actual figure. Although they collected data on both permanent and temporary paupers (which were essentially parallels of the indoor and outdoor relief models previously described), they added those two figures together before making their adjustment and before differentiating genders and other pertinent statewide data.

As a result, I cannot tally complete regional data because the adjusted paupers cannot be assumed to be evenly distributed. In addition, no local differentiation of problems can be made between those receiving shelter and those receiving only aid. I can say that Tompkins County sheltered six paupers and provided seasonal or other temporary aid to another 17. Of those 23, 34.8% were male, 65.2% were female, and 47.8% were children under 16 years old. Additionally two out of every thousand persons were permanently pauperized for some reason (Yates,

1824/1971). Although this is not bad data, it does not allow the homeless to be separated from other local welfare recipients.

A common practice throughout contemporary New York State was to refuse to admit presenters who could not claim local residency to the local almshouses, sending them instead back to their last county of residency. Such transience was a problem for an additional five persons in Tompkins, meaning that 17.9% of presenters in the county were refused. The committee compiling the data made a strong case that removal of transient paupers actually cost roughly the same amount of money as sheltering them, but caused significantly more duress both to paupers and to providers, as well as law enforcement and other involved public officials. They recommended that such individuals just be absorbed into the local system for the good of all (Yates, 1824/1971).

Looking at Appalachian New York in 1822 as reported yields a needy population comprised of 397 individuals, 40.8% of them were permanent paupers, 59.2% were temporarily affected, 40.1% were male, 59.9% female, and 31.5% children. An additional 53 transients yields an 11.8% refusal rate. Again, this does not include any of the additional pauper estimate expected by the committee.

New York in total showed an 1822 total of 14,010 needy individuals, only 31.1% of who were permanently pauperized, while 68.9% sometimes needed help making ends meet. With the previously observed 40.8% permanent paupers in Appalachian New York, it is clear that there was already more opportunity outside of Appalachia than there was inside. It was observed that 47.8% of state totals were male, 51.2% female and 44.4% children. There was only a 6.3% refusal rate. The adjustment did not affect the percentages of permanent to temporary, or the male to female ratios by more than 0.2%, but the numbers of children and transients received different adjustments. The result was a drop to only 39.6% of the population being children, and an increase to an overall refusal rate of 7.5% of presenters. There is a significant, but not a gross variance in the two parallel ratios available.

The transient population is likely estimated too high in any case due to the fact that no adjustment is indicated for the transferring of presenters within state lines, or the likelihood that many such highly mobile individuals would have been transported multiple times back to the same locality that clearly could not help them. Any pauper seeking aid in his or her home town and then one or more additional towns or counties would have been counted in each location, potentially several times within a year. Given this observation, it is likely that there would have been a clear decrease in overall expense if the suggestion to retain them in the Home to which they presented was accepted.

The additional data worked up by the Secretary's office from the adjusted totals provides that 36.25 % of all paupers helped were of foreign birth. Although there are no racial figures included, given that this set of data are from pre-Civil War, what few Black citizens who were reduced to asking for aid at this time were likely categorized in this number. Pursuing Nash's (2004) research previously discussed, the majority of those termed foreign would be among those who had fulfilled labor contracts entered into in exchange for travel to this country, or who had spent their meager savings on such passage in a gamble for a better life that did not materialize as hoped.

Among the permanent paupers, it was determined that 23% were in such a state because they themselves were alcoholics. An additional 45.8% were the victims of the alcoholism of those heads of household, making alcohol by far the most common cause of homelessness in the state. Disability was a problem for 11.6% of the permanent paupers, and an additional 4% were handicapped by blindness. Elderly citizens comprised 14.2%; and, 6.5% displayed the mental disabilities of idiocy or lunacy (Yates 1824/1971). Given the above demographics, at least 5.1% of presenters had multiple reasons for becoming homeless. Since that study claims 25.9% were able to work, the number of those with multiple problems is likely higher. The prevalence of alcoholism guarantees that dual diagnosis would have been frequently cited as the primary cause of homelessness if it had been suggested to contemporary statisticians.

The saddest statistic gleaned from this report is that 83.2% of the permanently pauperized children were paupers only because they were the children of alcoholics. Additionally, 66.7% of temporary relief went to families and individual children during the year (Yates 1824/1971). Given this sort of statistic, it is no wonder that so many groups later jumped at the chance to send missionaries to Southern and Central Appalachia as a means to address these same issues before they aspired to the levels once experienced by a developing New England.

As a final consideration of the New York historic record, it was interesting to note that the 1822 report encouraged communities to create County Homes and work houses as a means to reduce the overall cost of caring for the poor. Such homes, they claimed would add up to 20 years to the lives of those so afflicted by placing them in a clean and sanitary environment wherein they could be well fed, enjoy the company of others, and find recreational as well as occupational pursuits (Yates, 1824/1971).

By 1857, the Select Committee was appalled that such institutions were dingy, dilapidated and frequently un-cleaned facilities that breed sloth and disease, with the more troublesome inmates often confined in their own filth. They believed that the advent of specialized state institutions would ease that problem by removing some of the more problematic clientele and reducing the local per capita cost of care while providing more compassionate specialized care to those who needed it (New York State Select Committee, 1857/1976). One hundred years later, state institutions would be closing. Once again, the change would allegedly be for the good of the patients.

Maryland's Historical Record.

Maryland established the county home model of caring or its paupers by law in 1768 (Horton, 2007). Baltimore having long having established a routine involving state institutions, the county homes as they developed fell into step from the start, despite a lack of clear and consistent oversight from the state. The Prisoners' Aid Association took it upon itself in 1870 to annually inspect almshouses in addition to prisons and local jails, reporting their findings to county officials. The Governor established the State Board of Health and charged it to inspect all public institutions whenever called upon to do so. The first such request came in 1876 and will be discussed below. Ten years later, the State Lunacy Commissioner was established to inspect all institutions operating in the state that housed the insane, including almshouses. That Commission was also answerable to the Governor (Horton, 2007). An attempt to create an overarching entity for the purpose of visiting charities and penal institutions "was soon abandoned from the fear that the board would be made up with too great regard for politics and place" (Horton, 2007, n.p.).

Throughout the 1880s, a concerted effort was made to minimize the presence of children in county almshouses and state institutions not designed specifically in mind Horton, 2007. Although the benefits were undoubtedly innumerable to the children in terms of education and moral safety, the reasoning behind Maryland's focus was borne of the same fears that had the North Carolina State Board of Charities and Public Welfare snapping photos of every example of marginal stereotype they could find for their 1922 report.

There are only three counties in Appalachian Maryland today; and, at the time of the 1876 State Board of Health Inspection, the last of them, Garrett, had only recently been formed. As with the state as a whole, the other two made good use of state institutions, residency in which was charged in part to the counties from which their wards came (Chancellor, 1901). Alleghany County already counted 35 individuals on its paupers list, with only 12 of them living in the County Home. The other 23 were divided between the State Hospital, Mt. Hope Retreat, and Monteview. None among the 35 was mentally fit. There were at least three children living in the Home (Chancellor, 1901). It is not clear if it was these three children alone, or some other circumstance that led to the opening in 1883 of The Home for Friendless Children, but something in the Home shocked the legislature into action (Horton, 2007). All but one of the Alleghany paupers were White, and over half of them (54.3%) were male (Chancellor, 1901).

Washington County's pauper role was both more diverse, and significantly larger. There were 110 sheltered in the County Home itself, with an additional ten insane sheltered at either Monteview or Mayland Hospital. Twenty-nine of the Home's inmates were mentally unfit, raising the total to 39 (32.5%). Only 12.5% of those in the Washington County Home were colored (Chancellor, 1901), as compared to 25% of the statewide general population (Horton, 2007). All together, there were 155 paupers in Appalachian Maryland in 1877. Nearly half (47.7%) of those were mentally unfit. Coloreds as a sub-group were less likely to be designated as such at only 20%. Nearly two-thirds of those paupers were male (65.2%). Only 56.8% of the mentally unfit were male, leaving women more likely to be labeled as such. Conversely, of the 16 colored in the region, only three were mentally unfit, and two of them were male.

Conclusions

By the early twentieth century, when North Carolina was claiming the forefront of caring for the unfortunate (NCSBoPC, 1912), States were pushing for the dissolution of local facilities in favor of modern regional facilities that offered semi-specialized care to complement more state institutions. The federal government was beginning to administer various prevention-focused welfare programs that further reduced the need for care outside of one's own home. For all that New Deal programs accomplished in addressing the Great Depression, they also finalized the separation of aid from locality in rural areas by forcing cities to accept transients into urban shelters. Racial segregation within those shelters was effectively a compromise to outright discrimination via refusal to serve non-whites (Sutherland & Locke, 1971).

From the 1960s, extending through the 1980s, the federal government pushed out many of those same state and regional institutions as contrary to individual rights, as the Civil Rights Movement finally ended the practice of enforced segregation. Existing programs were significantly shorn of funds as additional programs were created. Smaller communities began to see the need returning for those services they once offered even though they did not know how to reintroduce them without offending those who once would have footed the bill as a poor tax rider on their property taxes.

All of this has led to a situation wherein responsibility for results has been coalesced into the local or even individual level, while oversight and fiscal dependence has been elevated to the federal level. The two slopes passed each other sometime mid-century, when virtually no local help was available, and while the two World Wars and their accompanying economic booms both increased economic opportunity, and reduced the visible homeless population.

Although entering the cycle later, Southern states did not really learn from the mistakes of their Northern neighbors, seeking example rather in what could be done instead of in what should not. Appalachian communities were generally slower at adopting national suggestions for change, but ultimately followed state and nation to the same ends as their more mainstream, and usually more urban, contemporaries.

At least in North Carolina, when financial support was offered by larger entities, Appalachian counties more often bought in without much of a fuss. They gladly allowed state or federal taxes to foot all or part of the bill instead of counties or towns. The agencies in those towns and counties now frequently find their support the same way.

When it comes to documentation of homelessness issues, aside from archival of requisite reports, newspaper articles, and the occasional memoire or commemorative text, nothing seems to be generated of a lasting nature from within Appalachia. The only exceptions I accessed were an archive collection by the professors creating and administering The Housing and Feeding the Homeless Program at Cornell University, which was comprised of all of the above plus letters and syllabi, and an unpublished paper by one of my former employees at the Hospitality House. He, like me, wanted to see the work move forward, and encouraged it to be provided to future students conducting research.

CHAPTER V

CONCLUSION

When I began this thesis, I listed as my goal a dual purpose. The first of those was to begin to address the fact that no true comprehensive study of homelessness in Appalachia can currently be done effectively given the dearth of community studies in the region that include homeless specific data. Towards that end, the second objective was to create a chronology of homeless service provision in Watauga County, North Carolina and compare that history to other Appalachian communities.

There is only so much one thesis can do to rectify an absence of readily available comparable data. I will be the first to admit that I have attempted here to do much more than was reasonable, but I am in hope that the effort will prove worth it to future research. If others begin to make their findings available within the region, I will judge my efforts here a success. I have done direct research on 19 communities in seven Appalachian states. All of them corroborated some key findings towards regional trends. If you are reading these words, then I have done my first duty well.

Watauga County

Watauga has in many ways been an easy county in which to conduct this research. There were no extenuating circumstances to make it a difficult place in which to conduct a study of the material. The only exception was early courthouse fires, which destroyed much of the early record. Renovations of the current courthouse and the NC State Archives slowed research down a bit, but did not ultimately remove any sources from availability.

My prior professional career as a service provider was almost completely within the county's boundaries. Although floods and eminent domain caused many to have to give up their homes, there were no major disasters to cloud the ranks of the homeless. Additionally, the county is close to transitioning from a rural county to an urban one. Although that change is arbitrary, being able to interact directly within the urban/rural dichotomy helped many of the realities of serving the homeless in

Appalachia stand out much clearer.

Central to the dynamics of life in Watauga are the actions of two industries, both of which have produced and continue to maintain large transitional populations. Appalachian State University constitutes the county's largest employer and an attraction for roughly 15,000 students every year. Recreation, including tourism and an increasing percentage of ASU's promotional activity, draws significantly more individuals to the area, with roughly an equivalent number of individuals maintaining seasonal homes in the county for the purpose of facilitating those visits.

The combined effect of these transient populations is a housing population roughly 40% greater than the actual population, and a housing market that is 99% saturated at any given time. Such a market draws rents far greater than Fair Market for the majority of landlords. That is bad news for the roughly 60% of the year-round population that is struggling to make ends meet. It is even worse news for those who depend on shelter and housing subsidies to keep them warm and dry. With an official unemployment rate of 3.3% and an obviously large service industry base, the county, especially the towns of Boone and Blowing Rock, are also an employment draw for regional employees and budding entrepreneurs. Boone's location on the juncture of several highways requires the county's roads to serve those commuting to work in other urban centers nearby.

Watauga's nature as a developing urban center has made it a natural place for a shelter to form. When the Watauga County Home transitioned into the Watauga County Boarding Home during the 1940s, it almost immediately began accepting inmates from the surrounding counties. The facility was not destined to last, however. The efforts of the state to maintain control, but not responsibility, were keeping the County Commissioners at odds over how best to run that shelter; and, its Keepers were having a hard time keeping the old house out of disrepair.

The rerouting and upgrading of highway 421 made the area more accessible, and farming had already become much less profitable. The town of Boone was allowed to use part of the property as a landfill, and the property was ultimately parceled and sold off to various developers. The heart of the property has been dedicated to the use of a variety of human services, including the first boarding home, the first health department, and Caldwell Community College. It remains in the County's possession today. This shift towards development left the county with no poorhouse until the current panel of providers began to form in the late 1970s and early 1980s, even though community action agencies targeting a reduction of poverty, among other things, began developing roughly a decade earlier.

Shifting Responsibilities

Before outlining the modern era and Appalachia, I want to summarize the cycle of responsibility that has emerged throughout this thesis. In the early to mid-1800s, the care for most of the unfortunate was very much a local responsibility. That care was shared between local governments – either city or county, and the community – usually through its larger churches. Faith groups were at the core of such care, often aided by a variety of individuals desiring to lend a hand with some facet of the process. The Salvation Army emerged in the 1850s, first in Europe, then in the United States, and began offering shelters in big cities, and eventually, lesser services in smaller areas experiencing need.

Counties usually provided only outdoor aid until each deemed it necessary to start some variant of almshouse, usually after the state it belonged to was solidified in its borders. Tenant-style "boarders," with or without compensation beyond board or outdoor aid, show up in all early censes. These boarders may have been extended family, neighbors, drifters, or locals hired to ensure the success of the farm. When payment was involved, the fee sometimes went to the laborer directly or to the laborer's host family, having hired out the help as a means to stabilize its own household. Cities were much the same, the variances being primarily fewer and smaller farms, earlier poorhouses, and the ability and demand to leverage resources to erect such facilities even before the state or county was fully formed. Those hired out were also more likely to be providing servant class activity than subsistence level (Foucault, 1965).

In general, northern states were well in advance of southern ones as far as solidification and infrastructure were concerned, but after the Civil War, all states were expected to have constitutions that satisfied the Union and those who were formerly among the Confederacy had to have their constitutions approved by the newly emerged nation. As a result, southern states began to take a more active interest in the welfare of citizens in their territories, often correlated with a desire to pacify their more northerly neighbors. Counties that were not participant in the County Home system were encouraged to evaluate their need to become so, and to set aside land for that purpose. Non-governmental community activity was not directly interfered with, but slowed down in the wake of increased presence by local governments.

Meanwhile, the nation began encouraging states to begin offering specialized institutions for the care of sectors of its more unfortunate citizenry. North Carolina was still encouraging its counties to raise the standards of its local facilities and did not begin promoting the state-institution model until a generation before the emerging Great Depression became a national priority. North Carolina's brief attempt to begin regionally addressing concerns was set aside when New Deal programs began to be implemented, and settled into a stance of facilitating federal programs without pursuing its own.

Watauga County was then not yet hosting a large enough urban center to set up a national transient shelter. Most local and state governments took a step back from homeless care to follow and benefit from national programs as best they could. Many never returned to their former positions of responsibility in the post-Depression era. Watauga's Home was still stable and, North Carolina was content to continue promoting the national status quo.

The social disconnect that occurred was that local governments had begun to look up and out, expecting that federal and state governments were still looking towards the needs of the individual and offering their leadership in those regards. This left communities themselves to pick up the slack. Most of them continued waiting for the next step to be proffered as well.

Appalachia

Throughout Appalachia, County Homes for the Aged and Infirm were becoming more and more dilapidated and succumbing to the state-institution model. Some closed their Homes for good to avoid making costly repairs, while others opted to provide regional, mostly private, boarding homes that would allow unmet need among neighboring counties to be addressed. Counties were following the lead of the nation and focusing on economic development, leaving the specialists to run their state and regional institutions. Some of those early institutions had focused on racial segregation, and may have encouraged the concentration of minorities in the largest urban areas.

When it emerged that those specialists were spending most of their time justifying the existence of their own institutions and asking state legislatures to provide an adequate budget, the fiscal focus of administrations was programmatically to the detriment of client welfare, and a period of Deinstitutionalization ensued. Patients reverted to their hometowns for care, or were discharged to the streets of their former host cities. They were then either absorbed back into their families, parked "temporarily" in nursing homes and hospitals that were not set up to care for them properly, or left to flounder until whatever stability they had enjoyed in the institution crumbled, leaving them unable to subsist on their own, often to end up incarcerated.

Many of those not going directly to the streets soon ended up there or in cheap motels and apartments, when families and facilities discovered they could not care for them and adequate local alternatives were not emerging. Community Action Agencies (CAAs) and DSSs struggled to help communities develop appropriate outpatient services. Those CAAs developed primarily in urban centers of rural areas and focused on programming region-wide. Many subsequently became the regions first housing authorities. The housing authority in Tompkins County, New York, for example, is still called Tompkins Community Action.

Services that emerged later followed the same trend. Every shelter that responded to my survey serves multiple counties, with the exception of those in Ohio. All of the Ohio respondents were located in urban counties; thus, it is not clear from the survey if the phenomenon is peculiar to Ohio, or a result of reducing the catchment area in order to serve the maximum local clientele. The shelters visited in two different northern communities were also located in urban counties. The Red Cross shelter in New York primarily served those in only one county. The REACH shelter in Hagersville, Maryland formed to keep those on the streets from freezing, but was the only shelter in the county not refusing those originating outside its borders.

Shelters in the Appalachian region primarily formed in three ways: the earliest were formed by non-governmental organizations in urban areas; several formed later as additional shelters in large urban areas; and, more commonly, many shelters formed within the urban growth centers of rural areas during the 1980s, when the fallout of Deinstitutionalization was not yet under control. This last widespread response was precipitated when those with the least chance of competition were being kept marginalized by national policies and economic trends, including gentrification.

Overwhelmingly, shelters formed during this time were created out of the efforts of various community members coming together in response to unmet need they were witnessing in their communities. Prominently featured among them were faith groups, frequently in combination. Churches were often still donating administrative space in addition to funding at the time of my survey. Many of the other programs encountered in my research were formed during or since that time by the same community efforts.

Shelters almost always went on to request and accept funding in exchange for guidance from federal sources, including HUD and OEO. The guidance is usually seen as a blessing in that practices are standardized and most situations have been experienced before. The fact that conditions are not the same in all communities emerges as problematic primarily when it comes to maintaining funding, which requires a series of reports throughout the year requesting that the funding continue and justifying expenditures within pre-described categories.

In small agencies, the administrative time spent in making and tracking such justification can detract from the efficacy of program administration to the guests, especially when several such grants are necessary to ensure an adequate budget. Not one respondent to the region-wide survey averaged more than 17 people in a single program on any given night in 2005, making them all small agencies. All of them offered a variety of services in their communities eligible to be charged to and tracked for a grant. When I left the employ of Hospitality House in Watauga County, it made use of three such grants, all with different operating years.

Not surprisingly, staffs of the agencies in question do not have time to compile the community studies this research would like to have found. They usually manage to keep an internal history of the agency updated for the purposes of donor outreach. That agencies are amenable to the idea of more comprehensive research is clear from the fact that they readily share information with students and journalists promoting awareness of the issues their clients face. Even my unscheduled visit to REACH in Washington County, Maryland provided enough information that I left knowing more about that county's homeless programs than most people know about those in their own community. The fact that I was working on a thesis was reason enough to grant an improvised interview.

In college towns especially, it should be relatively easy to take the next step and make sure some of the research being done is made available to the larger public. Given the current prevalence of service learning and internships, the lines between student and volunteer are often blurred, but many of those in both categories are more than capable of honing their writing skills to the benefit of the agency, community and future researcher. For those already conducting research, simply sharing a copy with the subject agency could make sure that it would at least find a spot on a shelf for others to access.

Most of the counties offering shelters in Appalachia are, like Watauga County, developing rapidly. If the community spirit inherent in the development of those services is to be recorded, the time to do so is now, before the towns get so big that no one remembers, or the shelter has survived long enough that none of those who created it are left in the area to be interviewed.

In Watauga County, services are still distinct enough that agencies still all cooperate with each other. Although there is some competition for local resources, the existing programs are distinct enough that they do not compete directly with each other and do not begrudge each other their successes. This gives them strength and resilience, as well as each other for peer support. Just as clients of services need to retain or build up a social network, the providers of those services need to be able to depend on the same.

Many of the agencies in Watauga County are beginning to group together in various locations in and around the city of Boone. New agencies that will emerge as demand continues to grow will need to be able to connect to one of those groups if they want to minimize hard feelings that may develop when they begin to compete for funds. The primary thing that can slow down that increase in demand at this point is an increase in affordable housing, preferable coupled with stable, long-term measures that prevent those living on the edge from falling.

GLOSSARY OF TERMINOLOGY

Appalachia: A governmentally designated region containing 406 counties and overlapping thirteen states ranging from New York to Mississippi. It is named after the Appalachian Mountain chain, which it includes.

Appalachian Regional Commission: Entity set up in 1965 and charged with the task of promoting economic advancement of Appalachia through community action plans.

Board of Volunteers: An officially recognized group of people (usually three) who were committed to regular visits to the local jails, almshouses, etc. that were overseen by the State Board of Public Charities and its successor organizations. The primary function was to make report on the condition of the facility, grounds, and inmates.

Boarder: Individuals living in another's home and often providing help on the farm. They were usually displaced neighbors, extended family members, or drifters that had no holdings of their own.

County Home Model: System of generally addressing homelessness that grew out of early poor laws to include a local shelter to house anyone unable to maintain themselves or be maintained by a family. The system included no systemic attempts to recondition the abilities of its wards.

Deinstitutionalization: Period of time when the State-Institution Model of care for marginalized individuals collapsed amid concerns that the mentally ill were not receiving appropriate care or being upheld in their individual human rights. The period began during the 1950s and ended during the 1970s. The full effects of its lack of systemic orchestration were not felt until the 1980s when many of the nations mentally ill had exhausted all other options and succumbed to homelessness.

Downtown Coalition of Churches: Faith group directly responsible for the creation of Hospitality House in Boone, NC. Member churches of the group also offered unofficial shelter to those needing both homeless and domestic violence assistance prior to current agency availability, as well as crucial assistance in the establishment of Hunger Coalition's food pantry.

Fair Market Value: Calculation of what is considered a reasonable rent in a given location based on area incomes and market availabilities.

Food Bank: Collection facility for foods to be redistributed to food pantries in a defined region. A food bank ensures standards of quality and may strive for uniformity in availability. The term is sometimes used erroneously by food pantries.

Food Not Bombs: A volunteer program that is commonly established on various campuses nationwide to promote peace and equality through the reduction of food waste through community meal and redistribution efforts. No long-term successful chapters emerged in this study.

Food Pantry: Community level access point for food assistance to consumers.

Great Depression: Period of widespread American poverty in the late 1920s and early 1930s that placed individual economic welfare under the supervision of the national government. Solidified wage economy as dominant over subsistence living.

Home for the Aged and Infirm: An attempt to revamp the image of county homes for the 20th century through a name change.

Hospitality House: Drawn from biblical reference, the name Hospitality House is applied commonly nationwide to various institutions offering hospitality to the dispossessed or their families. In this thesis it refers to a specific shelter in Boone, NC.

Inmate: Resident of any governmentally funded institution. The term demonstrates the punitive perspective of the early poor laws that provided it.

Jungle, The: A camping area in the center of Ithaca, NY populated primarily by those who have chosen not to pursue a lifestyle conducive to stable long-term housing.

Keeper of the Poor: Oversight person charged by the county or city with ensuring paupers are adequately cared for. In Appalachian counties, this person usually also acted as the Superintendant of the County Home.

Letting: Sharing the skills or labors of any ward (pauper, slave, cattle, child) to another without direct compensation to the laborer.

Loaves and Fishes: A volunteer program common at churches least throughout Appalachia that provides a community meal for all comers without question. Those who can are asked to provide a small donation to offset costs of the food.

MECCA: Methodist, Episcopalian, and Catholic Community Action grew into the Downtown Coalition of Churches in Boone, NC. Both strove to provide various assistance targeting the less fortunate of the community.

Mothers' Aid: Mid-1920s program federally adopted from several local efforts that sought to keep families together in their own home while breaking the cycle of poverty. This was one of the earliest prevention programs in the USA (and a likely progenitor of modern welfare recipient stereotypes.)

New Deal: Collection of programs begun in the F.D. Roosevelt Administration in the 1930s designed to stimulate individual welfare as well as the national economy.

North Carolina Fund: Five year program begun in 1963 by Governor Sanford to combat issues of poverty. It's focus on community specific issues in 11 sites around the state provided the basis from which local community action agencies nationwide and the national office of economic opportunity developed.

Outdoor Relief: Local government funds or credit provided to individuals who could thereby continue to be maintained in their own home or that of a neighbor or relative.

Pauper: An individual who is unable to maintain fiscal responsibilities within a community to the level necessary to sustain him/herself or his/her family.

Poor Laws: System of addressing a variety of marginal populations prone to becoming impoverished that began developing in Europe in the 1500s. Usually carried punitive characteristics.

REACH: Religious Effort to Assist and Care for the Homeless - A faith-based ministry that exists in many communities to make a variety of services more consistently available to those who need them.

Region D: One of several intermediary zones in North Carolina providing regional oversight of social development operating between the state and local level. Region D includes Watauga County, the primary research site of this thesis.

Revolving Door of Homelessness: The cycle of unsustainably addressing the housing needs of an individual, which allows them to repeatedly need to be re-served. Sometimes this is a result of poor skills management on the individuals part, but at least as often, it is a result of not identifying and addressing the true needs of the individual by the system of service in place.

Rural: For this research, the term is simplified for application at the county level to any county with fewer than 50,000 year round residents.

Sherwood Forest: Unofficial name of a common downtown camping area used by those unable to get into the shelter in Boone, NC until at least 2004.

Sleeping Place: Name of the program administered by the Downtown Coalition of Churches to overnight assistance to all seeking shelter. It was not until Hospitality House acquired a second property for the purpose of seasonal shelter that the name became associated with a permanent location.

State Board: The contemporary state-wide oversight board responsible for charitable institutions.

State Institution Model: Replaced the County Home Model and ultimately failed for the same fiscal and social inefficiencies it claimed to be addressing.

Superintendant of County Home: Onsite supervision of inmates of the county home and farm.

TEFAP: The Emergency Food Assistance Program is offered by the USDA through Second Harvest Food Bank in much of the nation. The foods are those that are not needed to ensure the adequacy of the school lunch program.

Transient: Anyone not consistently residing in a community in the long-term. For this research it usually means either the student population or the recreational one.

Urban: In order to be applied at the county level, the term is simplified to any county with a year-round population of 50,000 or more for this research.

War on Poverty: A more nebulous 1960s attempt to continue the efforts of the New Deal. The establishment of the Appalachian Regional Commission during this time legitimized both Appalachia and its culture of poverty in the national perspective.

Watauga County: The primary research site covered by this research. It is located in the north western corner of North Carolina, proximate to Tennessee and Virginia.

REFERENCES

Arthur, J. P. (1976). *A History of Watauga County, North Carolina with Sketches of Prominent Families*. Easley, SC: Southern Historical Press. (Original work published 1915).

Associated Press. (2008, May 27). Food banks facing new clients, mounting costs. *The Herald Mail*, p. A6.

Bradshaw, M. (2002). A political approach to regional development. In P. J. Obermiller & M. E. Maloney. (Eds.), *Appalachia: Social Context Past and Present* (4th ed., pp. 318-331). Dubuque, IA: Kendall/ Hunt Publishing Company.

Brown, E. (2001, September 20). Down and out in Ithaca with no roof over your head. *The Ithacan*, n.p. [electronic version]. Retrieved May 17, 2007 from http://www.ithaca.edu/ithacan/articles/0109/20/accent/0down_and_out.htm.

Brown, R. M. (1928). *Public Poor Relief in North Carolina*. Raleigh, NC: Edwards and Broughton Company for UNC Press, Chapel Hill.

Brown, W. E. (1997). *Recollections and Reflections*. Boone, NC: Parkway Publishers.

Bureau of the Census, Department of Commerce & Labor. (1906). *Paupers in Almshouses 1904*. Washington, DC: Author.

Cerese, R. (Director), & Channing, Steven. (Executive Producer). (2008). *Change Comes Knocking: The Story of the North Carolina Fund* [Motion picture]. Durham, NC: Video Dialog, Inc.

Chancellor, C. W. (1901). Report on the public charities, reformatories, prisons and almshouses, of the State of Maryland. In Gerald N. Gron (Ed.), *The State and Public Welfare in Nineteenth-Century America: Five Investigations, 1833-1877* (p. n.p. [Independent Pagination]). New York: Arno Press. (Original work published 1877).

City-Data.com. (2005). *Watauga County, NC- Detailed Profile* [Data Compilation]. Retrieved April 2, 2008 from www.city-data.com/county/watauga_county-NC.html.

Councill, W. B., & Hayes. (Eds.). (1882, pp. 368-369). *Untitled Deed*. (Available from Watauga County Deed Book J, Boone, NC).

Cuomo, M. (1983). *1933/1983 -Never Again* (Report to the National Governors' Association Task Force on the Homeless). Portland, ME: National Governors' Association.

Currie, R. D. (1998). *Appalachian State University, The First Hundred Years*. Prospect, KY: Harmony House Publishers Louisville.

Cutter, W. A. (1935). *Pioneering in Rural Rehabilitation in North Carolina*. Raleigh, NC: North Carolina Emergency Relief Administration.

Davis, D. E. (2000). *Where There Are Mountains: An Environmental History of the Southern Appalachians*. Athens: University of Georgia Press.

Department of Housing & Urban Development. (2006). [Mailing Lists]. Various Grant Recipient Lists. Retrieved March 8, 2006, from www.hud.gov.

Department of Housing and Urban Development. (2005). *Annual Performance Report Form*. Retrieved February 25, 2006, from www.hud.gov.

Diversity Task Force. (2007). *Appalachian Total Enrollment by Classification, Race and Sex Fall 2002-2006* (S13TotEnrollClassSexRace). Boone, NC: Appalachian State University. Retrieved March 07, 2008, from www.appstate.edu/www_docs/depart/irp/factbook/factbook0607/S13TotEnrollClassSexRace.pdf.

Dunaway, W. A. (2003). *Slavery in the American Mountain South*. New York: Cambridge University Press.

Eason, J. (2007, December 13). Boone Post Office muralist dies at 100. *The Mountain Times*, n.p. [electronic edition]. Retrieved December 15, 2007 from http://www.mountaintimes.com/mtweekly/2007/1213/muralist.php3.

Erikson, K. T. (1976). *Everything in its Path: Destruction of Community in the Buffalo Creek Flood*. New York, NY: Simon and Schuster.

Fair Market Rents.org. (2007, August 27). *Fiscal Year 2008 Final Fair Market Rents for Existing Housing* (Excerpt of Schedule B for Federal Report of the same name). Washington, DC:

universallivingwage.org. Retrieved March 15, 2008, from www.universallivingwage.org/fmrtables_2008/NC_FMR2008.HTM.

Fitchen, J. (1991). On the Edge of Homelessness: Rural Poverty and Housing Insecurity. *Rural Sociology, 57*(2), 173-193.

Foucault, M. (1965). *Madness and Civilization: A History of Insanity in the Age of Reason.* New York, NY: Vintage Books.

Geismar, E. (2007, November 8). Living below the line. *The Ithacan.* [electronic version]. Retrieved March 28, 2008 from http://theithacan.org/am/publish/news/200711_Living_below_the_line.shtml.

Getman, L. (2007, March). Homeless in Ithaca: Faculty member Gossa Tsegage '76 makes a documentary about "The Jungle." *ICView.* [electronic version]. Retrieved May 17, 2007 from http://www.ithaca.edu/icview/2126.

Ginn Resorts at Laurelmor. (2008). *Real Estate.* Ginn Corporation. Retrieved July 17, 2008 from www.laurelmor.com.

Grand, J. S. (2001). A Study of an Innovative Approach to the Delivery of Mental Health Services in Rural Appalachia: The RHOP in Perry County, Kentucky (Doctoral dissertation, The Wright Institute, 2001). *Dissertation Abstracts,* 64.

Hagaman, T., & A. J. Critcher. (1876). *Untitled Bid and Bond Contract for Thomas Hagaman.* Unpublished document, Watauga County Commission, Watauga County, NC. Retained by North Carolina State Archives. *Miscellaneous Records: Independent –Water.* Raleigh, NC.

Henbest, D. (2008, May 14-20). With food prices up, area food pantries find themselves in need. *Ithaca Times,* pp. 3-4.

Herald Mail Staff. (2008, May 27). REACH shelter seeks people to prepare bagged lunches. *The Herald Mail,* p. A7.

High Country Back Roads. (2006). *High Country Backroads Southern Loop* [Brochure]. Retrieved October 16, 2008, from www.highcountybackroads.com.

High Country Council of Governments. (2008). Retrieved August 28, 2008, from www.regiond.org.

Hopper, K. (1988). More than passing strange: Homelessness and mental illness in New York City. *American Ethnologist, 15*(1), 155-167.

Hopper, K. (2003). *Reckoning with Homelessness.* Ithaca, NY: Cornell University Press.

Horton, C. (Ed.). (2007). *Poor House Laws, Pre-1901.* Genealogy Trails History Group. Retrieved May 17, 2008, from http://genealogytrails.com/mary/poorhouselaws.html.

Hospitality House Shelter Staff. (2005 rev.). *History of the Hospitality House of the Boone Area, Inc.* Unpublished manuscript. Boone, NC.

Housing and Feeding the Homeless Records, #28\1\3161. (1996). Cornell University Library, Division of Rare and Manuscript Collections.

Hunger Coalition Staff. (2005 rev). [History of Hunger and Health Coalition]. Unpublished oral History of Joan Chater - March 17, 1999.

Landesman, L. Y. (2001). *Public Health Management of Disasters: The Practice Guide.* Washington, DC: American Public Health Association.

The Learning Web. (2007). 2007 Independent Living Survey Project: Identifying and Understanding the Needs of Homeless Youth In Tompkins County, New York. In Tompkins County Youth Services Department. Family Life Development Center (Ed.), *Independent Living Survey Project* (Summary of Findings, September 24, 2007). Ithaca, NY: The Learning Web.

Levine, M. (1981). *The History and Politics of Community Mental Health.* New York: Oxford University Press.

Local Development Districts. (n. d.). Appalachian Regional Commission. Retrieved April 2, 2006, from http://arc.gov/index.do?nodeId=14.

Lorance, N. (2006). *Post Office New Deal Artwork.* New Deal/ WPA Art in North Carolina. Retrieved August 11, 2008, from www.wpamurals.com/ncarolin.htm.

Madden, C. H. (1966). The war over poverty. *Law and Contemporary Problems, 31*(1): 45-63.

Mance, I. (2005). *Homeless in the High Country: A Profile of Homelessness: 1994-2004.* Unpublished master's research, Appalachian State University, Boone, NC.

McDonald, M. (1982). *TVA and the Dispossessed: The Resettlement of Population in the Norris Dam Area*. Knoxville: University of Tennessee Press.

Mechanic, D. (1994). Establishing Mental Health Priorities. *The Millbank Quarterly, 72*(3), 501-514.

Metropolitan Area Standards Review Committee. (2000). *Final Report and Recommendations from the Metropolitan Area Standards Review Committee to the Office of Management and Budget Concerning Changes to the Standards for Defining Metropolitan Areas*. Washington, DC: Office of Management and Budget.

Munn, R. F. (1965). The latest rediscovery of Appalachia. *Mountain Life and Work, 40*, 10-12. Berea, KY: Berea College.

Nash, G. B. (2004). Poverty and politics in early American history. In Billy G. Smith (Ed.), *Down and Out in Early America* (pp. 1-37). University Park, PA: The Pennsylvania state University Press.

National Coalition Against Domestic Violence (U.S.). (2004). *National Directory of Domestic Violence Programs: A Guide to Community Shelter, Safe Home, and Service Programs* (2004 Edition ed.). Washington, DC: Author.

New York State Select Committee Appointed to Visit Charitable Institutions Supported by the State. (1976). Report of Select Committee Appointed to Visit Chartable Institutions Supported by the State, and all County Poor and Work Houses and Jails. In Gerald N. Gron (Ed.), *The State and Public Welfare in Nineteenth-Century America: Five Investigation, 1833 - 1877* (pp. 1-153 [independent pagination]). New York: Arno Press. (Original work published 1857).

Nicholson, S. (2006a, June 01). Ginn Rep. Addresses Wake Up Watauga. *The Mountain Times*. [electronic edition]. Retrieved July 17, 2008 from http://mountaintimes.com/mtweekly/2006/0601/ginn.php3.

Nicholson, S. (2006b, December 21). Residents Suggets (sic) Residents Cannot Afford Watauga County. *The Mountain Times*. [electronic version]. Retrieved anuary 2, 2007 from http://mountaintimes.com/mtweekly/2006/1221/afford_wat.php3.

Noll, S. (1995). *Feeble Minded in Our Midst: Institutions for the Mentally Retarded in the South, 1900-1940*. Chapel Hill: University of North Carolina Press.

Norris, S. (2007, March 22). OASIS, WAMY Unveil Plans for Community Resource Center. *The Mountain Times*. [electronic edition]. Retrieved August 2, 2008 from http://www.mountaintimes.com/mtweekly/2007/0322/oasis_wamy.php3.

North Carolina Board of Public Charities. (2002). *First Annual Report of the Board of Public Charities of North Carolina. February 1870* (Melissa. Meeks, Ed.). Chapel Hill: University of North Carolina Press. (Original work published 1870) [electronic version]. Retrieved February 22, 2008 from http://docsouth.unc.edu/nc/char1870/char1870.html.

North Carolina Clerk of Superior Court. (1969). *Watauga County Trust Funds and Accounts for Indigent Children, 1915-1968* (Vol. A. 1915-1949). Raleigh, NC: NC Dept of Archives and History, Division of Archives and Manuscripts.

North Carolina Department of Archives and History. (microfilmed 1969). *Watauga County Appointments of Administrators, Executors and Guardians* (Vol. A 1873 -1926). Raleigh, NC: NC Dept. of Archives and History, Division of Archives and Manuscripts.

North Carolina State Board of Charities and Public Welfare. (1918). *Biennial Report of the State Board of Charities and Public Welfare, July 1, 1136 To June 30, 1918*. Raleigh, NC: Author.

North Carolina State Board of Charities and Public Welfare. (1920). *Biennial Report of the State Board of Charities and Public Welfare, July 1, 1918 To June 30, 1920*. Raleigh, NC: Author.

North Carolina State Board of Charities and Public Welfare. (1922). *Biennial Report of the State Board of Charities and Public Welfare, 1920-1922*. Raleigh, NC: Josephus Daniels, State Printer & Binder.

North Carolina State Board of Charities and Public Welfare. (1924). *Biennial Report of the State Board of Charities and Public Welfare, July 1, 1922 To June 30, 1924*. Raleigh, NC: Author.

North Carolina State Board of Charities and Public Welfare. (1926). *Biennial Report of the State Board of Charities and Public Welfare, July 1, 1924 To June 30, 1926*. Raleigh, NC: Author.

North Carolina State Board of Charities and Public Welfare. (1928). *Biennial Report of the State Board of Charities and Public Welfare, July 1, 1926 To June 30, 1928*. Raleigh, NC: Author.

North Carolina State Board of Charities and Public Welfare. (1930). *Biennial Report of the State Board of Charities and Public Welfare, July 1, 1928 To June 30, 1930*. Raleigh, NC: Author.

North Carolina State Board of Charities and Public Welfare. (1932). *Biennial Report of the State Board of Charities and Public Welfare, July 1, 1930 To June 30, 1932*. Raleigh, NC: Author.

North Carolina State Board of Charities and Public Welfare. (1934). *Biennial Report of the State Board of Charities and Public Welfare, July 1, 1932 To June 30, 1934*. Raleigh, NC: Author.

North Carolina State Board of Charities and Public Welfare. (1936). *Biennial Report of the State Board of Charities and Public Welfare, July 1, 1934 To June 30, 1936*. Raleigh, NC: Author.

North Carolina State Board of Charities and Public Welfare. (1938). *Biennial Report of the State Board of Charities and Public Welfare, July 1, 1936 To June 30, 1938*. Raleigh, NC: Author.

North Carolina State Board of Charities and Public Welfare. (1940). *Biennial Report to the North Carolina State Board of Charities and Public Welfare, July 1, 1938 To June 30, 1940*. Raleigh, NC: Edwards and Broughton Company.

North Carolina State Board of Charities and Public Welfare. (1942). *Biennial Report of the North Carolina State Board of Charities and Public Welfare, July 1, 1940 To June 30, 1942*. Raleigh, NC: Edwards and Broughton Company.

North Carolina State Board of Charities and Public Welfare. (1944). *Biennial Report of the North Carolina State Board of Charities and Public Welfare, July 1, 1942 To June 30, 1944* (The Information Service, Ed.). Raleigh, NC.

North Carolina State Board of Charities and Public Welfare. (2003). *Biennial Report of the State Board of Charities and Public Welfare, December(sic) 1, 1920 to June 30, 1922* (Biennial Report). Chapel Hill: University of North Carolina at Chapel Hill. Retrieved from http://docsouth.unc.edu/nc/charities1922/charities1922.html.

North Carolina State Board of Public Charities. (1870). *North Carolina Board of Public Charities First Annual Report, February 1870* (First Annual Report). Raleigh, NC: Author.

North Carolina State Board of Public Charities. (1891). *Report of the Board of Public Charities of North Carolina (1889-1890th ed.)*. Raleigh, NC: Josephus Daniels, State Printer and Binder, on the presses of Edwards and Broughton.

North Carolina State Board of Public Charities. (1892). *Annual Report of the Board of Public Charities of North Carolina, 1890-1891*. Raleigh, NC: Author.

North Carolina State Board of Public Charities. (1893). *Biennial Report of the Board of Public Charities of North Carolina, 1891-1892*. Raleigh, NC: Josephus Daniels, State Printer and Binder, on the presses of Edwards and Broughton.

North Carolina State Board of Public Charities. (1894). *Biennial Report of the Board of Public Charities of North Carolina, 1893-94*. Raleigh, NC: Josephus Daniels, State Printer and Binder, on the presses of Edwards and Broughton.

North Carolina State Board of Public Charities. (1895). *Annual Report of the Board of Public Charities of North Carolina, 1893-1894*. Raleigh, NC: Author.

North Carolina State Board of Public Charities. (1896). *Annual Report of the Board of Public Charities of North Carolina, 1894-1895*. Raleigh, NC: Author.

North Carolina State Board of Public Charities. (1897). *Annual Report of the Board of Public Charities of North Carolina, 1895-1896*. Raleigh, NC: Author.

North Carolina State Board of Public Charities. (1898). *Annual Report of the Board of Public Charities of North Carolina, 1896-1897*. Raleigh, NC: Author.

North Carolina State Board of Public Charities. (1899). *Annual Report of the Board of Public Charities of North Carolina, 1897-1898*. Raleigh, NC: Author.

North Carolina State Board of Public Charities. (1901). *Annual Report of the Board of Public Charities of North Carolina, 1899-1900*. Raleigh, NC: Author.

North Carolina State Board of Public Charities. (1902). *Annual Report of the Board of Public Charities of North Carolina, 1900-1901*. Raleigh, NC: Author.

North Carolina State Board of Public Charities. (1903). *Annual Report of the Board of Public Charities of North Carolina, 1901-1902*. Raleigh, NC: Author.

North Carolina State Board of Public Charities. (1904). *Annual Report of the Board of Public Charities of North Carolina, 1902-1903*. Raleigh, NC: Author.

North Carolina State Board of Public Charities. (1905). *Annual Report of the Board of Public Charities of North Carolina, 1903-1904*. Raleigh, NC: Author.

North Carolina State Board of Public Charities. (1906). *Annual Report of the Board of Public Charities of North Carolina, 1904-1905*. Raleigh, NC: Author.

North Carolina State Board of Public Charities. (1907). *Annual Report of the Board of Public Charities of North Carolina, 1905-1906*. Raleigh, NC: Author.

North Carolina State Board of Public Charities. (1908). *Annual Report of the Board of Public Charities of North Carolina, 1906-1907*. Raleigh, NC: Author.

North Carolina State Board of Public Charities. (1909). *Annual Report of the Board of Public Charities of North Carolina, 1908*. Raleigh, NC: E. M. Uzzell and Co., State Printers and Binders.

North Carolina State Board of Public Charities. (1910). *Annual Report of the Board of Public Charities of North Carolina, 1908-1909*. Raleigh, NC: Author.

North Carolina State Board of Public Charities. (1911). *Annual Report of the Board of Public Charities of North Carolina, 1910*. Raleigh, NC: Edwards and Broughton Printing Company, State Printers.

North Carolina State Board of Public Charities. (1912). *Annual Report of the Board of Public Charities of North Carolina, 1910-1911*. Raleigh, NC: Author.

North Carolina State Board of Public Charities. (1913). *Annual Report of the Board of Public Charities of North Carolina, 1911-1912*. Raleigh, NC: Author.

North Carolina State Board of Public Charities. (1914). *Annual Report of the Board of Public Charities of North Carolina, 1912-1913*. Raleigh, NC: Author.

North Carolina State Board of Public Charities. (1915). *Annual Report of the Board of Public Charities of North Carolina, 1913-1914*. Raleigh, NC: Author.

North Carolina State Board of Public Charities. (1916). *Annual Report of the Board of Public Charities of North Carolina, 1914-1915*. Raleigh, NC: Author.

North Carolina State Board of Public Charities. (1917). *Annual Report of the Board of Public Charities of North Carolina, 1915-1916*. Raleigh, NC: Author.

North Carolina State Board of Public Welfare. (1946). *Biennial Report of the North Carolina State Board of Public Welfare, July 1, 1944 To June 30, 1946* (The Information Service, Ed.). Raleigh, NC: Author.

North Carolina State Board of Public Welfare. (1948a). *Biennial Report of the North Carolina State Board of Public Welfare, July 1, 1946 To June 30, 1948*. Raleigh, NC: Author.

North Carolina State Board of Public Welfare. (1948b). *County Home Residents in North Carolina* (Information Bulletin No. 9). Raleigh, NC: Author.

North Carolina State Board of Public Welfare. (1950). *Biennial Report of the North Carolina State Board of Public Welfare, July 1, 1948 To June 30, 1950*. Winston-Salem, NC: Author.

North Carolina State Board of Public Welfare. (1952). *Biennial Report of the North Carolina State Board of Public Welfare, July 1, 1950 to (sic) June 30, 1952*. Raleigh, NC: Author.

North Carolina State Board of Public Welfare. (1954). *Biennial Report of the North Carolina State Board of Public Welfare, July 1, 1952 To June 30, 1954*. Raleigh, NC: Author.

North Carolina State Board of Public Welfare. (1956). *Biennial Report of the North Carolina State Board of Public Welfare, July 1, 1954 To June 30, 1956*. Raleigh, NC: Author.

North Carolina State Board of Public Welfare. (1958). *Biennial Report of the North Carolina State Board of Public Welfare, July 1, 1956 To June 30, 1958*. Raleigh, NC: Author.

North Carolina State Board of Public Welfare. (1960). *Biennial Report of the North Carolina State Board of Public Welfare, July 1, 1958 To June 30, 1960*. Raleigh, NC: Author.

North Carolina State Board of Public Welfare. (1962). *Biennial Report of the North Carolina State Board of Public Welfare, July 1, 1960 To June 30, 1962*. Raleigh, NC: Author.

North Carolina State Board of Public Welfare. (1964). *Biennial Report of the North Carolina State Board of Public Welfare, July 1, 1962 To June 30, 1964*. Raleigh, NC: Author.

North Carolina State Board of Public Welfare. (1966). *Biennial Report of the North Carolina State Board of Public Welfare, July 1, 1964 To June 30, 1966*. Raleigh, NC: Author.

North Carolina State Board of Public Welfare. (1968). *Biennial Report of the North Carolina State Board of Public Welfare, July 1, 1966 To June 30, 1968*. Raleigh, NC: Author.

O'Berry, A. L. (1936). *Emergency Relief in North Carolina: A Record of the Development and the Activities of the North Carolina Emergency Relief Administration 1932 - 1935* (J. S. Kirk, Cutter, & Thomas W. Morse, Eds.). Raleigh, NC: North Carolina Emergency Relief Commission.

Office of Economic Opportunity. (2005). *Annual Performance Report Form*. N. C. Department of Health and Human Services. Retrieved February 22, 2005 from www.dhhs.state.nc.us.

Ostwalt, C. E., Jr. (1992). Crossing of cultures: The Mennonite brethren of Boone, North Carolina. *Journal of the Appalachian Studies Association, 4,* 105-112. Boone, NC: Appalachian Consortium Press.

Patty, Rev. J. C. (1914). *Life of Lucius Bunyon Compton: The Mountaineer Evangelist*. Cincinnati, OH: Revivalist Press.

Reece, E. (2006). *Lost Mountain: A Year in the Vanishing Wilderness*. New York: Riverhead Books.

Regional Business Services Team. (2005). Watauga County Workforce In-Depth. In *Economic and Workforce Development Summit* NC: High Country Workforce Development Board. [electronic version]. Retrieved August 22, 2008 from http://www.regiond.org/esc%20data/watauga.pdf.

Rothbard, M. N. (Series Ed.), & Rockwell, L. H., Jr. (Vol. Ed.). (2004). *The Daily Article* (1544th ed.) [The Myths of Reaganomics]. Ludwig von Mises Institute. (Original work published 1988) Retrieved October 14, 2008, from www.mises.org/story/1544.

Sanders, H. (2005, November 3). Fighting poverty one week at a time. *The Appalachian*.

Sanford, T. (1966). Poverty's challenge to the states. *Law and Contemporary Problems, 31*(1), 77-89.

Schotz, A. (2007, November 6). Cold-weather shelter opens for new season of protection. *The Herald Mail*. [electronic version]. Retrieved May 5, 2008 from http://www. herald-mail.com/?module=displaystory&story_id=178501&edition_id=2001& format=html.

Sherlock, E. B., MD. (1911). *The Feeble minded: A Guide to Study and Practice*. London: Macmillan and Co., Ltd.

Snow, D., Baker, S., & Martin, M. (1986). The myth of pervasive mental illness among the homeless. *Social Problems, 33*(5), 407-423.

Starr-Stilling, G-E. (1998). *A Brief History of OASIS: Weaving an Ever Stronger Safety Net from Community Involvement*. Unpublished Document, OASIS, Boone, NC.

Sutherland, S., & Locke, H. J. (1971). *Twenty Thousand Homeless Men: A Study of Unemployed Men in the Chicago Shelter*. New York: Arno Press. (Original work published 1936).

Takeuchi, D. T., & Kim, K. F. (2000). Enhancing mental health services delivery for diverse populations. *Contemporary Sociology, 29*(1), 74-83.

Talley, B. S., & Coleman, M. A. (1992). The chronically mentally ill: Issues of individual freedom versus societal neglect. *Journal of Community Health Nursing, 9*(1), 33-41.

Thomas, M. P. (1968). *A Guide to Public Welfare in North Carolina*. Chapel Hill: The University of North Carolina Press.

Tollett, J. H. (1992). *Effects of a Nursing Home Intervention With Homeless Veterans: A Dissertation*. Knoxville: University of Tennessee Psychology Department.

U. S. Census Bureau. (1995a). *Population of Counties by Decennial Census: 1900 to 1990* [Edited and Compiled by Richard L. Forstall]. Retrieved September 2, 2007 from http:\\www.censtats.gov.

U. S. Census Bureau. (1995b). *Urban and Rural Definitions*. Washington, DC: U. S. Census Bureau. Retrieved August 22, 2008 from http://www.census.gov/population/censusdata/urdef.txt.

U. S. Census Bureau. (2000). Tompkins County New York 2000 American Community Survey. In *US Census Bureau American Fact Finder Fact Sheet* (Data Profile Highlights). Washington, DC: U. S. Census Bureau. [electronic version]. Retrieved February 17, 2008 from www.factfinder.census.gov.

U. S. Census Bureau. (2000). Watauga County North Carolina: 2000 American Community Survey. In *US Census Bureau America Fact Finder Fact Sheet* (Data Profile Highlights). Washington, DC: U. S. Census Bureau. [electronic version]. Retrieved February 17, 2008 from www.factfinder.census.gov.

U. S. Census Bureau. (2006). Tompkins County New York: 2006 American Community Survey. In *US Census Bureau American Fact Finder Fact Sheet* (Data Profile Highlights). Washington, DC: U. S. Census Bureau. [electronic version]. Retrieved February 17, 2008 from www.factfinder.census.gov.

U. S. Department of Commerce. (1994). The urban and rural classifications. In Economics & Statistics Administration (Eds.), *Geographic Areas Reference Manual* (pp. 12.1-12.24). Washington, DC: Bureau of the Census.

USA Counties Resident Population (April 1) 2000 (Complete Count) (13Sept2002nd ed.). (2002). Washington, DC: US Census Bureau. [electronic version]. Retrieved September 2, 2008 from www.censtats.census.gov.

Vissing, Y. M. (1996). *Out of Sight, Out of Mind: Homeless Children and Families in Small-Town America.* Lexington: University Press of Kentucky.

Washington Square United Methodist Church. (2007, December). *REACH Caregivers.* In Washington Square United Methodist Church (Newsletter).

Watauga County Commission. (1887, April). *Grand Jurors Report, April Term 1887* (Condition of County Buildings). Watauga County, NC: Unpublished Report Held by NC State Archives. Miscellaneous Records, Independent - Water. Raleigh, NC.

Watauga County Deeds Office. (n.d.). Keeper of the poorhouse (county home) 1891-1899 (broken series), 1930, 1932. In North Carolina State Archives (Series Ed.) & Watauga County Deeds Office (Vol. Ed.), *Watauga County Officials' Bonds, 1873 - 1958, Clerks - Mayors* (No. C.R.102.103.1, pp. 235 &c). Raleigh, NC: North Carolina State Archives. (Original work published 1892).

Watauga County Deeds Office. (n.d.). Keeper of the poorhouse (county home) 1891-1899 (broken series), 1930, 1932. In North Carolina State Archives (Series Ed.) & Watauga County Deeds Office (Vol. Ed.), *Watauga County Officials' Bonds, 1873 - 1958, Clerks - Mayors* (No. C.R.102.103.1, p. 273). Raleigh, NC: North Carolina State Archives. (Original work published 1893).

Watauga County Deeds Office. (n.d.). Keeper of the poorhouse (county home) 1891-1899 (broken series), 1930, 1932. In North Carolina State Archives (Series Ed.) & Watauga County Deeds Office (Vol. Ed.), *Watauga County Officials' Bonds, 1873 - 1958, Clerks - Mayors* (No. C.R.102.103.1, n.p.). Raleigh, NC: North Carolina State Archives. (Original work published 1931).

Watauga County Deeds Office. (n.d.). List of Paupers 1876. In North Carolina State Archives (Series Ed.) & Watauga County Deeds Office (Vol. Ed.), *Miscellaneous Records, No Date, 1858, 1872-1974 Independent - Water [Box 3]* (No. C.R.102.928.3, n.p.). Raleigh, NC: North Carolina State Archives. (Original work published 1876).

Watauga County Quick Facts [2006 census estimates]. Washington, DC. Retrieved August 22, 2008 from quickfacts.censuss.gov.

Watauga County Registrar of Deeds. (1955). [Platt Book 002, page 079]. Unpublished platt records. Document ID: 19550711000000070.

Watauga County Registrar. (1960). *Watauga County Book of Session Minutes, Docket 8 1940-1960.* Unpublished manuscript, Watauga County Deeds Office, Boone, NC.

Westview Special Studies in Contemporary Social Issues (Series Ed.), & Fitchen, Janet M. (Vol. Ed.). (1981). *Poverty in Rural America: A Case Study.* Boulder, Colorado: Westview Press.

Whisnant, A. M. (2006). *Super-Scenic Motorway: A Blue Ridge Parkway History.* Chapel Hill: University of North Carolina Press.

Winkler, W. M. (1945, May 24). Notice of sale of real estate. *Watauga Democrat*, p. 2.

Wright, J. D. (1988). The mentally ill homeless: What is myth and what is fact? *Social Problems,* *35*(2), 182-191.

Wynne, W., Jr. (1938). *Five Years of Rural Relief.* Washington, DC: Works Progress Administration-Division of Social Research.

Yates, J. (1971). Report of the Secretary of State in 1824 on the relief and settlement of the poor. In David J. Rothman (Ed.), *Poverty, U.S.A.: The Historical Record; The Almshouse Experience: Collected Reports* (pp. 939-1137+). New York: Arno Press & The New York Times. (Original work published 1824).

Zawisza, K. (1996). Homelessness is serious in rural areas. In David. Bende & Bruno. Leone (Series Eds.) & Tamara L. Roleff (Vol. Ed.), *The Homeless: Opposing Viewpoints* (No. Opposing Viewpoints Series, pp. 52-89). San Diego, CA: Greenhaven Press, Inc. (Original work published 1991)

APPENDIX A

Summary of Poor Laws as Relevant to Watauga County

North Carolina was a beneficiary, as were all of the former colonial states, of the system often referred to as "the poor laws." These were inherited primarily from England before the Revolutionary War, but continued to evolve for decades thereafter, incorporating contemporary trends from throughout Western Europe and America. The essential components of the poor laws were that:

- The inability of family and friends to care for an individual caused such responsibility to fall upon the local jurisdiction.
- Those who were able to labor should do so;
- Each local jurisdiction (generally the county) was responsible for those that had residency therein; and that
- Residency was determined within a jurisdiction by the prior existence of a stable home for a period of time – most often one year, frequently up to three.

In order to implement such requirements, the County Commission of each area was empowered to administer a poor tax from which poor relief was to be paid. Each county was encouraged to maintain a County Home under the supervision of the County Commission. These were generally directly maintained by a "Keeper of the Poor." The facilities were subject to routine state inspection and were obligated to provide adequate food, shelter, heat and raiment. The expectation of labor from the inmates was up to the local jurisdiction and based partially on the individual's ability to perform the required tasks. Table A lists some of the primary legislation that made treatment of the poor what it is today.

Table A-1: *Evolution of Legislation Concerning the Poor and Homeless*

Year	Source	Summary
1536	O'Berry	Statute of Henry XVIII: precursor to poor laws; established joint responsibility for poor by requiring government and church care of poor (without the commitment of public funds)
1572	O'Berry	Queen Elizabeth introduced poor tax, poor tax collectors, and overseers of the poor
1597, 1601	O'Berry	Codification of Poor Laws by British Parliament: provided that work would be provided for those who could work but couldn't find any; provided that those who couldn't work would be cared for by relatives if possible and local government otherwise; those who wouldn't work would be penalized; almshouse also established as catch-all facility; poor children would be apprenticed in order to learn a trade before they became mired in poverty
1777	Brown	Each NC county elects 7 freeholders as overseers of the poor for three year terms, two of whom become wardens; residency is set at one year
1779	Brown	Slave-owned livestock eligible for seizure and resale; half of proceeds go as bounty, the other half go towards care of poor
1785	Brown	Counties keeping state busy requesting permission to build poor houses; county government given permission to decide when and if appropriate without state involvement
1831	Brown	States still driven crazy by county requests; clarification of whom the requests should go to, as well as the right to include a farm, hire a superintendant, and contract to lowest bidder
1854	Brown	State codification of poor laws; non-residents to be removed to home location: residency in families tied first to father/husband, and second to mother if children illegitimate
1868	Brown	New NC constitution: establishes County Commission, which replace former Wardens; Keeper replaces former Superintendant; contract extended to 2 years; blacks become clearly eligible for care

c1868	Brown	BoPC formed by constitution hires Rev. Weller as Chairman found 6 counties didn't have homes, and two were unoccupiable due to construction and renovations: all but one were in Appalachia; no concept of separation of inmates was found - deemed doubly detrimental to children present
1872	Brown	Dr. C.T. Murphy replaces Weller, found only one County Home in better than horrible shape (Built by Gov. Morehead in Guilford); those in Appalachia essentially rotting, leaking, log cabins
1876	Brown	Letting of Paupers prohibited
1891	Brown	The Home for the Aged AND Infirm
1914	Brown	Woodrow Wilson Establishes National Commission to study national Vocational Education potential
1915	Brown	County Commissions no longer required to accept lowest bid for Keeper; supreme Court rules County Homes a necessary, but not mandatory, expense, eligible for the local issuance of bonds to raise construction funds
1917	Brown	Superintendant of Public Welfare created without clearly established function; solidification of state-wide organization by county
1923	Brown	Mothers' Aid Law
1932	O'Berry	Hoover denying federal responsibility for caring for poor; willing to allow loans to states; sees problem as inefficiency in making wealth available to all
1932	O'Berry	Reconstruction Finance Corporation ear-marks $300 million to allow states to create and implement job creation plans with federal help repayable through deductions from other federal grants for such things as highway construction
1933	O'Berry	Roosevelt passes Federal Emergency Relief Act (FERA), Civilian Conservation Corps as part of a plan to create jobs and promote the conservation and development of national resources

1934	O'Berry	FERA revamped to create Transient Division and reduce administrative costs: effectively separated responsibility of county governments from funds dispersal and ended former poor law system
1935	O'Berry	Emergency Relief Appropriation Act created WPA and Resettlement Act; the later took over absorbed and revised Rural Rehabilitation programs
1954	Madden	Vocational Rehabilitation Act
1962	Madden	Manpower Development and Training Act
1963	Madden	Vocational Education Act
	Cerese	Launch of the North Carolina Fund to attempt to alleviate poverty before homelessness occurred
1964	Madden	Economic Opportunity Act: Created the Office of Economic Opportunity
1965	Madden	Appalachian Regional Development Act: Appalachian Regional Commission and the War on Poverty

(Madden, 1982; O'Berry, 1936; Cerese & Channing, 2008; Brown, 1928)

APPENDIX B

Original Questions Asked of North Carolina County Homes

POOR HOUSE QUESTIONS

The following questions are provided as they were typed on pages 27 and 28 of the electronic edition of the First Annual Report of the Board of Public Charities of North Carolina, first published in February 1870 (NCSBoPC, 1870/2002). They constitute the first look at local homeless by the State of North Carolina.

1. Is there a poor house in your County? If not, what provision has been made for taking care of the poor?
2. How far is the poor house from the County seat?
3. State the number of buildings, size of each, and of what material built.
4. How many rooms in each building?
5. How are the buildings and rooms ventilated?
6. What are the means of protection against fire?
7. How is the supply of water furnished for drinking, cooking and bathing purposes?
8. How are the buildings heated in winter?
9. How many inmates can be accommodated with the present arrangement?
10. How many now in charge?
11. How many of these are able to work?
12. How many are helpless or bed-ridden?
13. How many are under involuntary confinement?
14. Give the names of all such, and the cause of confinement either here or on a separate list.
15. What is the daily average of food allowed to each inmate?
16. What is the average weekly cost of maintenance of each?
17. What is the name of the keeper or overseer of the poor house?
18. Is he industrious, sober and discreet?
19. What pay does he receive?
20. What is the name of the physician who attends the inmates?
21. How far does he reside from the poor house?
22. What pay does he receive for his services?
23. How many inmates were there in poor house July 1st, 1868?
24. How many admitted since that time?
25. How many deaths since that time, and of what diseases did they die?
26. How many discharges from other causes?
27. Give a general description of the premises. Are they well arranged, neat and in good condition, or dilapidated and out of repair?
28. How many acres of land belong to poor house tract, and what is the quality of the land?
29. How much is in cultivation?
30. What crops are raised on the land, and how are the products used?
31. What vegetables are raised for Summer and Winter use?
32. Are the houses and yard protected by shade trees?
33. Are the ashes and manures saved and used in improving the land?
34. Has any punishment been inflicted upon any inmate since admission? If so, who? By whom? What punishment? And for what offence?

APPENDIX C

Homeless Provider Survey 2006

Completed forms should be returned by April 4, 2006 to:
Carl Jenkins, Graduate Researcher, XXXXXXXXXXXXXXXX or call to fax: XXXXXXXXXXXX
Please base your answers on the last completed fiscal year.

SECTION 1: AGENCY INFORMATION (Regards this agency regardless of programs offered.)

Organization Name: _____

Mailing Address: _____ County: _____

Town/City: _____ State: _____ Zip: _____

Telephone: (_____) _____ FAX: (_____) _____ ☐ Call before faxing?

E-Mail: _____ Website: _____

Executive Director: _____

Name of Person who can answer questions about this report: _____

Title: _____ Phone/email: (_____) _____ /_____

....

I hereby certify that information reported here is true and accurate to the best of my knowledge, and
that the information reported may be used in academic, scholarly, and published materials except
where otherwise noted in the survey.
Do not publish: ☐ staff names. ☐ program names ☐ organization names ☐ anything.
Signature of Authorizing Individual _____ Title _____
Printed Name of Authorizing Individual _____
Phone/Email: (_____) _____/_____ Date: _____

....

1. The Agency's Fiscal Year is: ☐ July – June. ☐ January – December. ☐ Other: _____

2. This organization (or chapter) was founded in _____. (Month/Year)

3. This organization was incorporated in ____. (Date: MM/YYYY) ☐ Same ☐ Not incorporated

4. It serves homeless persons in (region covered) _____

5. Were there key groups involved in founding the organization? ☐ No ☐ Yes _____
   *such as coalitions, churches, agencies, government entities, etc.

6. When are your business hours? _____
   *When can a person knowledgeable about your agency or programs be contacted in the offices?

7. How many shelter programs do you operate in the region? _____

8. Does the current board membership of the applicant organization include at least one homeless or
formerly homeless representative? ☐ No ☐ Yes

9. Are clients given other opportunities to participate in the administration of the
program/organization? ☐ No ☐ Yes, Explain: _____

SECTION 2: PROGRAM INFORMATION

Many organizations operate several distinct programs. If you operate several programs under one umbrella, please list them below. You may also fill out the survey for each individual program if you prefer.

First Program Name: _____ Town/ County (if different): _____
Program Director: _____ Phone/ e-mail: (____) _____
If different than the parent organization, when was this program begun? _____
....

Second Program Name: _____ Town/ County (if different): _____
Program Director: _____ Phone/ e-mail: (____) _____
If different than the parent organization, when was this program begun? _____
....

Third Program Name: _____ Town/ County (if different): _____
Program Director: _____ Phone/ e-mail: (____) _____
If different than the parent organization, when was this program begun? _____
....

Fourth Program Name: _____ Town/ County (if different): _____
Program Director: _____ Phone/ e-mail: (____) _____
If different than the parent organization, when was this program begun? _____
....

10. Which types of programs do you offer for the homeless in your area?

☐ Crisis Shelter   ☐ Transient Shelter   ☐ Domestic Violence
☐ Day Shelter/ Drop-in   ☐ Night shelter   Center
Center   ☐ Transitional Shelter   ☐ Safe Haven
☐ Emergency Shelter   ☐ Permanent Shelter
☐ Orphanage or Group Foster Home   ☐ Other (Please describe): _____

11. What populations are served by this organization?

☐ General Homeless   ☐ Transitioning (former homeless receiving sup

☐ Chronic Homeless   ☐ At risk of homelessness (homeless prevention

☐ Domestic Violence   ☐ Single Adult Males   ☐ Children only

☐ Families   ☐ Single Adult Females   ☐ Infants only

☐ Single Parent Families only → ☐ Male Head of Household only-- ☐ Female Head only

☐ Other (Describe) _____

12. Do you ☐ own, ☐ lease, or ☐ receive donated use of the property your program operates on?

12b. If use is donated, who owns the property? (Town, County, Church, Civic Group, etc.)
Comments: _____

SECTION 3: SERVICES OFFERED

Please answer the following questions relate to the services offered by the organization.

13. How does a prospective client request assistance? (Walk-in, Hotline, Sheriff, Referral, etc...)

_____

14. Do you charge for your services? ☐ No ☐ Yes (How much?) 14b. $ _____ per _____
    14c. How many free days are standard? _____ ☐ none ☐ n/a
    14d. How are the fees used? _____ ☐ n/a

15. Presuming compliance, what is the maximum length of stay? _____ 16. Average Stay _____
What is your: 17. average daily occupancy? _____ 18. average annual bed-night count? _____
19. How often did you exceed capacity during the report year?
    ☐ Never ☐ Occasionally ☐ Frequently ☐ Often ☐ Always

20. Is this a cyclical occurrence? ☐ No ☐ Yes. Explain: _____

21. How do you deal with overflow?
☐ Turn them away   ☐ Refer to another   ☐ Motel space
☐ Make space anyway   shelter
☐ Use another building   ☐ Never happens
Explanation, if necessary: _____

22. Does the program reserve or prioritize services based on criteria not addressed above? Such as by disability/ies, presenting problems, gender, race, religion, participation in education or doctrinal sessions, etc. ☐ No ☐ Yes (please describe) _____

23. In addition to shelter, which of the following services did you offer or provide during the report year?

Service Category		
☐ Outreach	☐ Housing counseling	☐ Showers/ Baths
☐ Case management – general guidance	☐ Housing placement	☐ Hygiene dispensary/ closet
☐ Crisis Intervention	☐ Employment counseling	☐ Clothing dispensary/closet
☐ Pursue Entitlement Benefits	☐ Employment referrals	☐ Clothing referrals
☐ Life skills training	☐ Employment training	☐ Meals for applicants
☐ Alcohol / drug counseling	☐ Employment placement	☐ Soup Kitchen
☐ Alcohol / drug treatment	☐ Child care	☐ Nutrition counseling
☐ Mental health counseling	☐ Transportation –local fare	☐ Debt Assistance- outstanding balances
☐ Mental health treatment	(bus, tram, cab, etc.)	☐ Debt Assistance- Homeless prevention
☐ HIV/AIDS-related services	☐ Staff Driven Assistance	☐ Debt Absorption- Move-in expenses
☐ Other health care services	☐ Car gift or cheap purchase	☐ Other (please specify)
☐ Education	☐ Relocation/ Travelers Aid	
☐ Education guidance	☐ Legal Counseling	Comments:
☐ Housing referrals	☐ Legal Dispute Settlement	
	☐ Laundry	

SECTION 4: PERSONS SERVED

Try to count each person entering your program only once, even if they returned to your program multiple times in the reporting period. *If you receive federal funding through ESG or HUD, many of these answers may be found in your Annual Reports to those programs.*

24. How many total guests did you record entering during the reporting year? _____
     24b. Does this number include dependant children? ☐ No ☐ Yes ☐ n/a

Please fill out the following charts to the extent possible.

25. How many persons entered your program from the following areas during the reporting year?

	Singles not in families		Families		
	Males	Females	Males	Females	
Adults 62 +					
Adults 51 - 61					
Adults 31- 55					
Adults 18 - 30					
Youth 13 - 17					
Youth 6 - 12					
Youth 1 - 5					
Infants					
Totals	____	____	____	____	Family units
How many are chronically homeless?					Family units

How many persons entered your organization from the following Races and Ethnicities during the year?

26. Races	Total	27. Ethnicities	Total
Native American		Hispanic/Latino	
Asian		Non-Hispanic/Latino	
Black/African-American		Unknown	
Pacific/Hawaiian Islander		Other	
Caucasian			
Unknown			
Other			

28. How many of your guests were Veterans? _____
    28b. How many of your total Veteran clients were chronically homeless? _____
    28c. How many of your total Veterans were women? _____

29. What was the primary reported reason for homelessness for your guests? Please choose only one per person.

Cause	**Total**		Disability	
Developmental or Mental			Alcohol abuse	

Drug abuse		Unemployment	
Dual Diagnosis		Underemployment	
Release from an institution*		Domestic Violence/ Sexual Assault	
Natural disaster		Abused youth	
Eviction		Other youth (Runaway)	
Relocation		Other (please specify)	
Transient			
Chronic Health/Disability			

*If a participant came from an institution but was there less than 30 days, count them according to their situation prior to the institution. Theoretically, a short institutional stay shouldn't be enough to cause someone to become homeless without a more pressing issue, but a longer stay might create a homeless situation.

30. How many folks had the following employment situations when they entered your program?

	Employment Status	Entry			Employment Status	Entry
a.	Full time			d.	Temporary Agency	
b.	Part Time			e.	Unemployed	
c.	Training Program			f.	Unemployable	

31. Prior Living Arrangements: Where did you receive your guests in this program from?

Location	Total		
Non-sheltered (street, park, etc.)		Substance Abuse Treatment*	
Emergency Shelter		Psychiatric Facility*	
Transitional Shelter		Jail/ Prison*	
Relative's Home		Hospital*	
Friend's Home		DV Situation	
Rental housing		Other (Specify)	
Homeowner			
Location	Total		

SECTION 5: FINANCIAL INFORMATION

This last page relates to financial data. Some agencies with multiple programs track them separately and some do not. Some methods of tracking finances will make this piece hard to provide. Please feel free to provide the data on each program if preferable.

32. What percentage of your budget comes from the following sources? In cases where funds are administered by other organizations, please consider funds based on their origins. (If your state administers federal funds, please consider them as from a federal source.)

	Source	%
a.	Grants and other Sponsorships	
b.	Local Government	
c.	State Government	
d.	Federal Government (please specify)	
e.	Foundations/ Trusts	
f.	United Ways	
g.	Community Support/ Fundraisers	
h.	Program charges (rents/ fees)	
i.	Other	
	Total	**100%**
j.	In-Kind, non-essential (or all if no tracking)	
k.	In-Kind, offsetting costs (if differentiated)	
	Adjusted Total (>100%)	

33. Which of the following describes the size of your budget before in-kind donations?

☐ less than $50,000   ☐ 100,001 – 250,000   ☐ 500,001 - $1 million
☐ 50,000 - 100,000   ☐ 250,001 – 500,000   ☐ more than $ 1 million

34. Which of the following describes the size of your paid staff in Full-time equivalents (FTEs)?

☐ 1 - 2 FTE   ☐ 6 - 10 FTE   ☐ 21 – 50 FTE
☐ 3 - 5 FTE   ☐ 11 - 20 FTE   ☐ over 50 FTE

SECTION 6: OTHER PROVIDERS IN YOUR REGION

35. Can you help me identify other homeless service providers in your region?
☐ There are no other homeless providers in the area besides us and DSS.

(Please provide organization names, and contact persons, emails, phones or mailing addresses as available. Do not list physical addresses of shelters that have non-disclosed locations.)

Organization Name	Contact Information (May be address, phone, e-Mail and/or a person.)
Services Provided:	
Service/s Provided:	
Service/s Provided:	
Service/ Provided:	
Service/s Provided:	
Service/s Provided:	
Service/s Provided:	

36. If you wish not to have your contact information shared with other service providers in the region, please check here. ☐

Thank you very much for your time and thoughts! -cdj

Additional comments and/or evaluations:

APPENDIX D

Sample Emergency Shelter Intake Evaluation

On the following pages is a reproduction of the form created to document all guests at Hospitality House of the Boone Area incorporated. It was a compilation of the form we were using when I joined the staff of Hospitality House in 1996 and the Annual Performance Reports (APR) required to be filed with the Department of Housing and Urban Development and the Office of Economic Opportunity in exchange for grants received. Service coordination (aka case management) time spent with almost every sheltered client could be counted towards the requirements of one or the other of the grants.

Our original form consisted of lettered questions aimed at addressing each client's needs in relation to stability, health, and safety. Where those questions were not also asked by one of the granting agencies, they retained their original designations, such as: question "A. Employment status upon entrance." Those questions that were asked by the grant received for transitional shelter guests were given the corresponding number in the APR, such as: Question "10: Prior living situation." The commonly accepted responses were likewise assigned the letter ascribed by the grant worksheet.

In many cases, the two grants asked the same questions, but in different orders, or with different ascriptions to expected answers. In such cases, each response would have a parenthetical designator after the response telling the demographer where to tally the response for the other grant. For example, "8.Race, answer c. black/African American" is followed by '(E5b)' for Emergency Shelter Grant APR question 5, answer b.

Every year, some questions changed on one APR or another, but with a blank updated form, the service coordinator compiling demographics could respond appropriately to every question on each grant, and three different intake or exit evaluation sheets were not necessary to maintain multiple programs. The agency could maintain consistency even when the needs and desires of the grantors changed. When a client changed programs, a new form was filled out to capture information that changed, such as a new location and admission date. Most information could be transferred from one document to the other before the client came in for the meeting.

For several years before I left the shelter, statewide discussion and efforts surrounded the desire to facilitate an electronic means of simplifying report generation for federally funded shelters. The new Homeless Management Information System (HMIS) would require OEO and HUD APRs to coordinate expected responses, age ranges, and similar concerns, while the overall system created a master list of questions that would ensure both sets of questions could be answered with just a few taps on the keyboard.

Original discussions were bogged down by the variety of questions homeless service providers needed answered in order to meet the needs of their respective clients. Several of us voiced concerns that the system was unwieldy and seemed to have the underlying purpose of minimizing funding by allowing additional reports on the state level to be generated based on client identification numbers. It was expected that such new reporting technology inherently overlooked the underserved, served but undocumented, and un-served populations. The results of using such flawed data to produce overarching statistics would not have been advantageous to those for whom the grants were designed to serve. The new system finally came on line after I was no longer a shelter director, so I am unable to evaluate as to how well hopes and fears were realized.

Intake/Exit Form

Section 1: *may be completed by any staff/ volunteer*

Guest #_____ (TBA) Program/Facility: Emergency Shelter
Entry Date:_____ Exit Date: _____
Total number in family unit _____

1. **Name**_____ SSN _____-_____-_____ **DLN** _____
(include state initials)

Other names: Include ALL maiden names, married names, first and last nicknames, former and current, etc.

_____

2. **Relationship:** ( ) single/self ( ) head of household (only one per family)
( ) child ( ) adult family member

| Additional Family Members / Cross-references: | | | |
Name	Relationship	DOB	SSN

For accompanied minors, this section is enough. For all others, complete additional form/s.

3. Are you able to interact with others in close quarters? ( ) Yes ( ) No(*ie. shelter confines*)

4. Are you able to accept some restrictions on your usual lifestyle? ( ) Yes ( ) No(*ie. guidelines, house rules*)

5a. **DOB** __ /__ /__ __ __ __ 5b. **Age** at entry _____

5c. **Gender** ( ) Male ( ) Female

6a. **Veteran?** Yes ____ No ____

6c. How long have you been homeless? _____ Homeless Situation: _____
6d. How many times have you been homeless? _____
6b. Chronically homeless person?* Yes ____ No ____

*An unaccompanied homeless individual with a disabling condition who has either been continuously homeless for a year or more OR has had at least four (4) episodes of homelessness in the past three (3) years. To be considered chronically homeless a person must have been on the streets or in an emergency shelter (i.e. not transitional housing) during these stays.

7. **Ethnicity**. Hispanic/Latino Yes ____ No ____ (E5c)

8. **Race**.
a. ____ American Indian/Alaskan Native (E5d) b. ____ Asian (E5a)
c. ____ Black/African American (E5b) d. ____ Native Hawaiian/Other Pacific Islander (E5a)
e. ____ White (E5e) f. ____ Other/Multi-Racial _____
E5g ____ Unknown

Staff Checklist:
( ) ID Copied for file ( ) Former Guest: date of last stay ___/___/____
( ) File Checked ( ) Discuss Re-entry
( ) Police Record Check ( ) Homeless Eligibility Guide Completed
( ) Guidelines signed & filed ( )Verification of homelessness attached

Note: numbers such as (E5b) refer to ESGP-APR variances from TS-SHP APR questions, which constitute most of pages 1, 3 & 5.

Intake/Exit Form

A. **Employment status** upon entrance
 a. Employed full-time, permanent (40 hours per week or more)
 b. Employed part-time, permanent (less than 40 hours per week)
 c. Employed full-time, temporary/seasonally
 d. Employed part-time, temporary/seasonally
 e. Not employed and not in any training/academic program
 f. Enrolled in training /academic program and employed
 h. Participating in an unpaid job experience/internship
 I. Homemaker
 j. not able to work

B. **Educational level**: Enter highest grade finished _____ Degree/s _____

C. Are **other agencies** now working with you? ( ) Yes   ( ) No
 If yes:

Agency	Contact	Phone	Release

D. Do you currently have a **Probation/Parole** Officer?
 name of PO:_____

 ( ) Obtained consent for release of information

E. **Medical**
 Current Medical Conditions

 Significant Past Medical History

 Current Medication/s *(all active scripts and dosages. Remind to update if there is a change.)*

F. **Allergies**:

G. **Emergency Contact**: _____ _____ (___)____-_____
                                    Name   Phone   Relationship

H. **Resident Status** _____
 ( ) a. Local Resident (lived in referring county >1 year)
 ( ) b. New Resident (lived in referring county < 1 year)
 ( ) c. Passing through

I. **Referring Counties**:
(Bolded entries are within our service area; Italics denote a recognized extended area; normal print denotes commonly used other entries.)

( ) **a. Watauga**	( ) **b. Avery**	( ) c. Ashe	( ) d. Wilkes
( ) **e. Caldwell**	( ) f. N.C. Resident	( ) g. Out of State	( ) h. Other (please specify)
( ) **i. Mitchell**	( ) **j. Alleghany**	( ) **k. Yancey**	
( ) l. Johnson, TN	( ) m. Carter TN	( ) n. Washington, TN	

Intake/Exit Form

Section 2: *may be completed by any staff/ volunteer*

9a. Special Needs/ Presented Problems. *Participants may have several.*

a. _____ Mental illness (E2Fa)		b. _____ Alcohol abuse (E2Fb)		
c. _____ Drug abuse (E2Fc)		d. _____ HIV/AIDS and related diseases (E2Fe)		
e. _____ Developmental disability (E2Fq or a)		f. _____ Physical disability (E2Fq)		
g. _____ Domestic violence/sexual assault (E2Ff)		h. _____ Other _____ (E2Fr,s...)		

E2Fd. _____ Dual diagnosis (a+b or a+c) E2Fg. _____ Unemployment
E2Fh. _____ Underemployment E2Fi. _____ Eviction
E2Fj. _____ Natural Disaster (fire, flood, etc.) E2Fk. _____ Runaway/ Homeless youth
E2Fl. _____ Abused/Neglected child E2Fm. _____ Juvenile delinquent
E2Fn. _____ Release from correctional facility (jail) E2Fo. _____ Transient (passing through)
E2Fp. _____ Relocated

10. Prior Living Situation. *Choose one.*

a. _____ Non-housing (street, park, car, station, etc.) b. _____ Emergency shelter
c. _____ Transitional housing for homeless persons d. _____ Psychiatric facility*
e. _____ Substance abuse treatment facility* f. _____ Hospital*
g. _____ Jail/prison* h. _____ Domestic violence situation
i. _____ Living with relatives/friends j. _____ Rental housing
k. _____ Other _____

Institutions should only be counted for stays greater than 30 days.

11a. Monthly Income.

_____ a. No income _____ b. < $150 _____ c. $151 - $250 _____ d. $251- $500
_____ e. $501 - $1,000 _____ f. $1001- $1500 _____ g. $1501- $2000 _____ h. > $2000

11b. Resources

_____ a. Supplemental Security Income (SSI) _____ b. Social Security Disability Income (SSDI)
_____ c. Social Security _____ d. General Public Assistance
_____ e. Temporary Aid to Needy Families (TANF) _____ f. State Children's Health Insurance Program
_____ g. Veterans Benefits _____ h. Employment Income (SCHIP)

_____ i. Unemployment Benefits _____ j. Veterans Health Care
_____ k. Medicaid _____ l. Food Stamps
_____ m. Other (please specify) _____ n. No Financial Resources

Completed by:_____ Date:_____

If not completed by a Service Coordinator
Reviewed by:_____ Date:_____
        Service Coordinator

Section 3: Exit Information: *Should be completed upon exit by a Service Coordinator.*

11c. Monthly Income.

_____ a. No income _____ b. < $150 _____ c. $151 - $250 _____ d. $251- $500
_____ e. $501 - $1,000 _____ f. $1001- $1500 _____ g. $1501- $2000 _____ h. > $2000

11d. Resources

_____ a. Supplemental Security Income (SSI) _____ b. Social Security Disability Income (SSDI)
_____ c. Social Security _____ d. General Public Assistance
_____ e. Temporary Aid to Needy Families (TANF) _____ f. State Children's Health Insurance Program
_____ g. Veterans Benefits _____ h. Employment Income (SCHIP)
_____ i. Unemployment Benefits _____ j. Veterans Health Care
_____ k. Medicaid _____ l. Food Stamps
_____ m. Other (please specify) _____ n. No Financial Resources

12. **Length of Stay** *(months)* _____ (weeks) _____ (days) _____
Z. **Employment status on exit** (see page 2,#A) _____

13. **Reasons for Leaving**. *If multiple reasons exist, clearly note the primary reason.*
a. _____ Left for a housing opportunity before completing program
b. _____ Completed program
c. _____ Non-payment of rent/occupancy charge
d. _____ Non-compliance with project
e. _____ Criminal activity / destruction of property / violence
f. _____ Reached maximum time allowed in program
g. _____ Needs could not be met by project
h. _____ Disagreement with rules/persons
i. _____ Death
j. _____ Other (please specify)
k. _____ Unknown/disappeared

14. Destination.

a. _____ Rental house or apartment (no subsidy)
b. _____ Public Housing
c. _____ Section 8
d. _____ Shelter Plus Care
e. _____ HOME subsidized house or apartment
f. _____ Other subsidized house or apartment
g. _____ Homeownership
h. _____ Moved in with family or friends (permanent housing)
i. _____ Transitional housing for homeless persons
j. _____ Moved in with family or friends (transitional shelter)
k. _____ Psychiatric hospital
l. _____ Inpatient alcohol or other drug treatment facility
m. _____ Jail/ Prison
n. _____ Emergency shelter
o. _____ Other supportive housing
p. _____ Places not meant for human habitation (e.g. street)
q. _____ Other _____
r. _____ Unknown

15. Supportive Services. *Services received during program.*

a. _____ Outreach
b. _____ Case management
c. _____ Life skills (outside of case management)
d. _____ Alcohol or drug abuse services (E6B3)
e. _____ Mental health services   (E6B2)
f. _____ HIV/AIDS-related services (E6B2)
g. _____ Other health care services   (E6B2)
h. _____ Education   (E6B4)
i. _____ Housing placement
j. _____ Employment assistance   (E6B1)
k. _____ Child care
l. _____ Transportation
m. _____ Legal
n. _____ Other _____
E6B6. _____ Nutrition support
E6B5. _____ Housing Placement

APPENDIX E

Early Contracts for Keepers of the Poor in Watauga County

The following three sets of documents related to the Watauga County Home were transcribed by me from photocopies of original county records located in the North Carolina State Archives. I preserved spellings and abbreviations as close to those presented as possible, but it is likely that many transcription errors have been made. The handwriting in the first set was especially difficult to read, and those penning the originals in 1891 and 1892 appear to have been uncomfortable with the legal language they were emulating. Blackburn was inserted after the original document had been completed, presumably because the expected bond was not able to be garnered from Long and Lovill without help. Lovill was also replaced between the recording and signing of the document by J. P. Councill.

North Carolina, Watauga County
Know all men by these presents, that we Riley Hodges principal and Calvin Long and E. F. Lovill & M.B. Blackburn as sureties are held and firmly bound unto the State of North Carolina in the sum of one thousand dollars, to the payment of which will and timely to be made We bind ourselves our heirs executors and administrators firmly by these presents, signed and sealed this the 9th day of Dec., 1891.

The conditions of the foregoing bond is such that whereas the above bounden Riley Hodges has been appointed by the Board of County Commissioners of Watauga County as the Keeper of the County Poor-House or Home for the Aged and infirm, and as such Keeper has agreed with the said Board of Com's in consideration of being appointed to said office as follows. The said Hodges agrees to furnish and sow all the grass seed needed to be sewed on the poor house farm. He is also to properly repair the fence on said farm from Holland Hodges line along the public road to Trivett's line and fence. He is also to clear off a field below Clarisa Councill's house and tend it for year 1892 said field contains some five to seven acres.

(sic) It's further agreed by the said Hodges Keeper as aforesaid not use any timber from the farm except dead timber from fair use. The said Hodges is to receive for keeping the inmates of the home in the following prices, for the helpless ($4.75), for all others ($3.00). He is also to have the proceeds of the farm. Now therefore if the said Riley Hodges shall well and faithfully discharge the duties of said office as Keeper as aforesaid as prescribed by law and account for and pay over all monies that come into his hands as law requires then this obligation is to be void otherwise to remain in full force and effect.

Witness	Riley X Hodges
Seal	
	His Mark
W. B. Councill, Jr.	Calvin Long
Seal	
James B. Councill	M. B. Blackburn
Seal	
	J. P. Councill
Seal	

Filed for Registration Jan the 4th 1892 and Registered in the Register of Deeds office of Watauga County in book of Official Bonds on page 235 & c.

Jan twentieth 1892
C.J. Cothill, Register of Deeds

We Calvin Long and E.F. Lovill and M. B. Blackburn, sureties to the aforesaid bond being duly sworn says each for himself that we is worth the sum hereafter set opposite his name over and above all his debts and liabilities, homestead, and personal property exemption.
Calvin Long $500.00
M. B. Blackburn $500.00
J. P. Councill $500.00

Sworn to and subscribed to before me this the 7th day of Dec 1891.
WC Todd DC [Deputy Clerk]

Riley Hodges Bond $500 Keeper of the home for the aged and infirm Approved Jany 4 -1892
J.H. Hart, C.B.C. [County Board of Commissioners]
W.C. Coffey
W.W. Presnell
(Watauga County Deeds Office, 1892, p. 235 &c)

This second document was considerably easier to transcribe, although some educated guesses of a couple words and intended spellings was necessary. The line inserted mid-text may have been provided to facilitate a signature. Dating to 1876, it was the earliest contract found relating to sheltered care of paupers in Watauga County.

State of North Carolina
Watauga County
Know all men by these presents that we Tho's Hagaman, A. J. Critcher are held and firmly bound unto the County of Watauga in the sum of $840 current money of the United States. To the true and faithful payment whereof we bind ourselves our heirs executors and administrators jointly and severally and firmly by these presents signed with our hands and sealed with our seals this October the 3rd Day A.D. 1876. The Conditions of this obligation is such that whereas the above bounden Tho's Hagaman _____ hath bid off and agreed to take the following paupers of said County. (viz) Malinda Keller, S.A. Black, Gilly Mitchell, Patty Thompson, Amos Mast (col), Eliz. Bridges, Fanny McGuire, Eliza and Susan Keeton, Catherine [Horton?], Eliza Penly, Andrew Bower, and [Jnr?] Church, for one year from this date. If the aforesaid Tho's Hagaman shall well and truly maintain and clothe and not otherwise mistreat the aforesaid paupers, then the above obligations to be null and void otherwise to remain in full force and effect.
Signed, sealed ~~and delivered~~ in presents of

A. F. Davis   Thomas Hagaman
Sealed
                                                            A. J. Critcher
Sealed
(Watauga County Deeds Office, 1876, n.p.)

The third set was again significantly easier to transcribe. Notice that space was left after Long's name to allow an insertion if necessary, and that the document itself was significantly neater than the earlier bond applied. Lovill is no longer included.

North Carolina
Watauga County

Know all men by these presents that we Riley Hodges as principal and J P Councill and Calvin Long sureties are held and firmly bound unto the State of North Carolina in the sum of One Thousand Dollars current money of the United States for the faithful payment of the same we bind our selves our heirs and assigns. Signed sealed and delivered in our presence this 4th day of December A.D. 1893.

The conditions of the above obligation is such that Riley Hodges was duly elected (or appointed) Keeper of the Home of the aged and infirm of Watauga Co. for 2 years from the 1st Monday in December 1893.

Now if the said Riley Hodges shall well and truly take care of and feed and clothe all the aged and infirm, who is now at the Home of the aged and infirm, and all who may be ordered to said Home by the Board of County Commissioners of said County, and do the work, and keep up the farm, and do all things according to a written contract entered into between said Hodges and the Board of County Commissioners now on file in the office of the Register of Deeds in Boone, now if the said Riley Hodges shall well and truly perform all of the duties aforesaid according to contract, then this obligation shall be null and void otherwise to remain in full force and effect.

Riley Hodges	Seal
J. P. Councill	Seal
Calvin Long	Seal

We the undersigned sureties swear that we are worth the amounts set opposite our names over and above our Homestead and personal property exemptions by law, and our indebtedness and liabilities.

Sworn to before me W. C. Todd D.Clerk   J. P. Councill $500.00
"   "   Joe B. Todd C.S.A.   Calvin Long
                    $500.00

Approved and ordered registered and filed as the law directs December 4th 1893
W. C. Coffey, chair Bd Co Com
H.H. Farthing \
                    | Coms
J. C. Horton   /
Filed Dec. 4th 1893 and Registered in the Register of Deeds office of Watauga Co in Book of Official Bonds on page 273 Dec 13th 1893 C.J. Cothill, Reg. of Deed

(Watauga County Deeds Office, 1892, p. 273)

ACKNOWLEDGEMENTS

There are many people who should be thanked for their contributions to bringing this thesis to fruition. First and foremost among them are my thesis committee members, not only for their guidance and editing, but also for their patience and perseverance. They are Dr. Sue Keefe of the ASU Anthropology Department, Dr. Brad Nash of the Sociology Department, and Dr. Patricia Beaver of the Appalachian Studies Program. Debbie Bauer similarly deserves eternal gratitude for the many services she provides all students in the department. Without her dedication to make life smoother, many of us would miss opportunities and deadlines, and generally spend much more time on day-to-day minutiae trying to catch up with basic requirements. Drs. Keefe and Nash also taught classes wherein I was able to explore various components of this research, as did John Alexander Williams and Fred J. Hay.

The Office of Student Research (OSR), the Cabbell Fund, the Capstone Scholarship Award, and the Center for Appalachian Studies, and the Graduate Student Association Senate (GSAS) all provided funds for this process or the presentation of various parts thereof. The Internal Review Board Staff and the Cratis D. Williams Graduate School provided oversight and permission to perform the research.

Father Chuck Blanck, Mary Ruth and Larry McCrae, Glenn Hodges, John Ward, Danielle Harrington, Jim Atkinson, Compton Fortuna, Crystal Winebarger, Grady Woodring, Robert Cox, Lori Watts, Tina Barse, Jill Parker, the Tompkins County Food Distribution Network, Lynne Mason, Ned Fowler, Amy Miller, Jennifer Herman, Angela Miller, Glenn-Ellen Starr-Stilling, Marian Peters, and the staffs of the various agencies herein discussed, have all directly added insight during the research phase of this discourse. Bill Paterson, Father Tim Smith, Pastor Wayne Brown, Betty Williams, Sherri Miller, and many others, some of whom remain anonymous, all gave insight and guidance into where to look for information, or simply encouragement to keep up the work.

Anne Jasper, Crystal Risbon, Ms. Barb, and Aslı Mete all gave editing assistance for parts of the document. As this thesis will hopefully prove useful for those in the field, it was helpful to have the benefit of eyes unaccustomed to grading papers give feedback on public comprehension and readability. Aslı Mete, James Jenkins, Bellavia, & Erin Aylor all became gracious and helpful hosts at various times during the research.

And to all my friends, colleagues, and classmates who let me run on about what I was doing despite the fact that there were more interesting things to discuss outside of classroom walls without ever once pointing out that I was "almost done" for at least six months, I thank you for not deserting me as well. If I have left anyone out by name that should have been included, I sincerely apologize.

www.ingramcontent.com/pod-product-compliance
Lightning Source LLC
Chambersburg PA
CBHW071350280526
45787CB00001B/271